I love getting a letter in my actual mailbox—especially if it's a personal letter from someone I know and love. Deb Burma's book *Joy* enables me to see the Book of Philippians not only as the apostle Paul's letter to the believers in the ancient city of Philippi but also as God's personal letter addressed specifically to me. Through the pages of Philippians and Deb Burma's study, I am encouraged and uplifted. Joy spills out of every page!
Sharla Fritz, author of *Enough*

Deb's thorough research of the Book of Philippians engaged me and continually refreshed me with JOY. Although the book is written to be read five days a week for eight weeks with weekly group studies, I found myself yearning to read more every day. Deb includes endearing personal stories that tie into Bible lessons. Not only does Deb delve deeply into Philippians, but other Scripture references in each lesson are listed alongside thought-provoking questions. Each page exudes JOY, teaching me there is JOY in absolutely everything: every situation, event, encounter, task, sadness, prayer, opportunity, and at every hour of every day. Deb illustrates JOY in JESUS! I now look for JOY in absolutely everything!
Connie Johnson, prayer warrior, educator, mentor

Deb Burma draws each reader into a three-way conversation with herself and St. Paul as she picks up on the apostle's celebration of the joy he has in the Lord and with the Philippian congregation. She leads readers through the epistle with personal stories, commentary on the text, and application of its truths to daily life. The study provides optional video introductions and cues for using the daily devotions in a weekly group study that enriches the individual's immersion in the conversation with Paul into which the Holy Spirit leads readers, sharing his joy at being Christ's own.
Robert Kolb, emeritus professor of systematic theology, Concordia Seminary, St. Louis

The treasures of this Bible study are sandwiched between Deb's opening illustration of a treasured personal correspondence of joy and her heart-to-heart letter of encouragement for joyful living at the close. She has a knack for reaching out and grabbing your hand with her words, and, whether you dive into this study on your own or with a group, you'll feel like you're doing it with a friend! "Special Delivery" explanations and study answers welcome new believers as well as the tired or burdened so that no one is left out of the conversation. Deb's inclusion of excellent application opportunities and "Joy Snapshots" provide for personal growth and inspire joyful words and actions for others!
Pat Maier, cofounder of Visual Faith Ministry, women's retreat facilitator, Camp Arcadia

Joy is a must-do study about the Book of Philippians. With her funny, relatable stories, Deb Burma encourages, delights, and teaches about the true JOY we have through Christ.
Come and see how you can become a woman of JOY—even in hard seasons of life. Through this in-depth study, you will better understand the humility, confidence, and contentment you have in Jesus, and how Paul shows these as JOY throughout the fascinating Book of Philippians.
Christina Hergenrader, author of *Family Trees & Olive Branches* and *Love Rules*

Are you ready for a joyful challenge? Well, this is a joy-filled epiphany! Each session is wrapped in prayer and overflowing with opportunities to discover joy in all circumstances. I appreciate the adaptability which allows for personal or group study while digging deep into Paul's Letter to the Philippians. I can't wait to share Deb's fresh look at this Letter of Joy with the sisters in Christ in my church Bible study group. Joy will be oozing out all around us!
Carol von Soosten, women's Bible study leader

Deb Burma's book *Joy* beautifully guides us through the Book of Philippians. She gives us forty days of delight, inviting us to embrace joy even in the midst of life's difficulties. In a faithful way, Deb keeps the focus on the great hope, the return of our Savior on HIS day! Through Paul's affection and encouragement to his readers, Deb helps us "sparkle like stars" in our world. Her "Special Delivery" notes enhance understanding of the text; each day a "Joyful Challenge" applies the verses to our lives. Whether studying *Joy* with a small group or reading it alone, you will be blessed!
Renee Gibbs, teacher, retreat speaker, encourager

Joy: A Study of Philippians is like opening up a heartfelt letter penned by a trusted and treasured friend. With warmth and wisdom, Deb Burma challenges and encourages the reader to examine Paul's timeless teachings to the Philippians. Easy to read and personal, with helpful "special deliveries" and relatable stories, Deb invites the reader into a deeper understanding of God's definition of *joy* through His Word. Thought-provoking questions allow the reader to consider joy through God's lens and not that of the world. And in doing so, just like Paul, we, too, can be genuinely filled with joy and find reasons to rejoice every day!
Carol Fedewa, director of women's ministry at Hales Corners Lutheran Church, Hales Corners, WI

Deb Burma guides the reader through forty celebratory days of discovery in the loving words of Paul to the Christians of Philippi—believers who needed the words of encouragement, grace, and joy just as much as we do. The theme of each chapter demonstrates the continuous message of our Father's grace, love, and joy. Deb's writing is honest and personal—an open conversation over a cup of coffee. I treasured each day of insight into the Word and eagerly awaited the next chapter. (Okay, I sometimes read two at a time!) How exciting to *LIVE* this letter to the Philippian Church with soul-filled grace and JOY!
Jan Struck, Christian speaker and humorist

Joy! It is the desire of our hearts to be joy-filled people of God. Deb Burma's *Joy: A Study of Philippians* is the perfect combination of daily devotion, personal reflection, and weekly gathering to spiritually grow and embrace a joy-filled life. You will be encouraged to put into practice the "joy-filled" learnings He is revealing to you. And that is truly transforming! I highly recommend this study to women's ministry leaders, neighborhood small groups, and coffee-shop women's meetups!

Gail Ficken, executive coleader, PLI

JOY

A STUDY OF PHILIPPIANS

DEB BURMA

CONCORDIA PUBLISHING HOUSE · SAINT LOUIS

Concordia
Publishing House

Founded in 1869 as the publishing arm of The Lutheran Church—Missouri Synod, Concordia Publishing House gives all glory to God for the blessing of 150 years of opportunities to provide resources that are faithful to the Holy Scriptures and the Lutheran Confessions.

Published by Concordia Publishing House
3558 S. Jefferson Ave., St. Louis, MO 63118-3968
1-800-325-3040 • cph.org

Peter Hermes Furian/Shutterstock
VerisStudio/Shutterstock

Manufactured in the United States of America

2 3 4 5 6 7 8 9 10   28 27 26 25 24 23 22 21 20 19

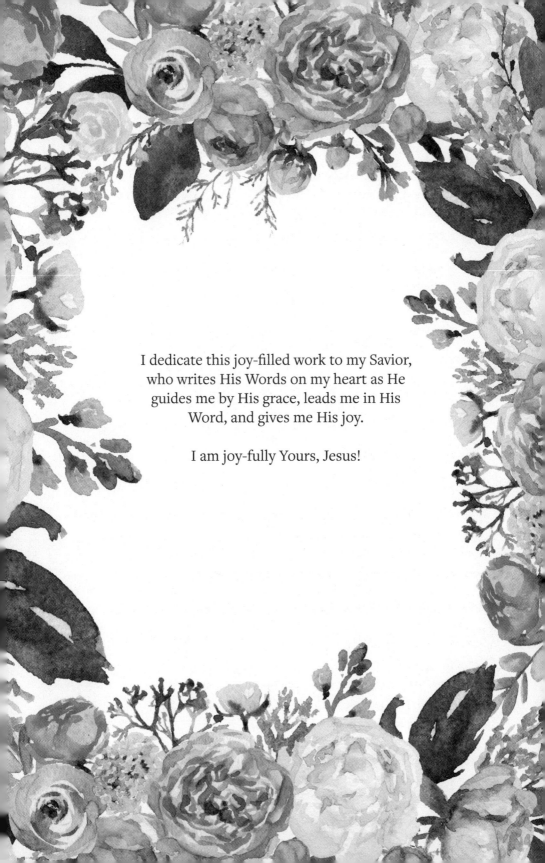

I dedicate this joy-filled work to my Savior, who writes His Words on my heart as He guides me by His grace, leads me in His Word, and gives me His joy.

I am joy-fully Yours, Jesus!

Table of Contents

Introduction

If you've mailed me a letter, I probably still have it. I treasure handwritten words because the writer has something special to say. Maybe the letter is filled with news and updates. Or perhaps it contains humbling words of thanks. Often, it includes encouraging words and tender reminders. Sometimes it contains carefully crafted remarks that challenge or hold me accountable. One of my favorite parts of personal letters is the valediction, the complimentary close, such as "Blessings, my friend," "With a grateful heart," or "Yours in Christ." Each closing expresses the heart of the writer, with honor and regard for the recipient, and often includes a word that conveys *relationship*, like "friend" or "yours." I keep all types of personal letters, emails, and social media messages and reread them when I need a good word or two.

You've received such a letter. Okay, probably many such letters, but I'm speaking of one in particular. The heart of the writer overflows with joy with each word. That writer is the apostle Paul, and while the first recipient was the Early Church he founded in Philippi, every word is penned personally for you and me too, as God the Spirit inspired the letter writer. We're about to embark on a forty-day adventure, reading and studying this letter that's often referred to as the Letter of Joy. Like other letters we may have received, it is chock-full of news, updates, and humble words of thanks. It's also bursting with encouragement and tender words of truth. And if you're ready for a challenge, this letter contains an exhortation of the best kind—to live a life worthy of the Gospel of Christ, by the grace of God!

In his Philippians commentary, R. C. H. Lenski writes, "Joy is the music that runs through this [letter], the sunshine that spreads over all of it" (Lenski, pp. 691–92). In fact, the words *joy* and *rejoice* are mentioned seventeen times in Philippians. As we read, I believe you'll see why.

The English language falls short in giving the word *joy* a worthy definition. When I asked Google to define joy, I received, quite simply, "a feeling of great pleasure or happiness." Is joy just an emotion? Is joy synonymous with happiness? My artistic friend tried to capture the essence of joy by giving us lots of words in an attempt to define it. Some come close, but others, not so much!

Some days, we may exclaim, "I am filled with joy!" Mountain-top moments are easy to recall: vacations and births, successes and weddings. Author Heidi Floyd said, "Really grand events are the easiest way to express the joys we've felt. The everyday is a much more difficult statement for joy, though, isn't it? We have routine, pressure, tasks, the mundane and monotonous that fill our every waking moment. A moment of joy has to shine fairly brightly to be noticed in the day-to-day operations of normalcy. I made a promise to myself a few years ago that I would find those joys on a daily basis" (Floyd, p. 73). Could you and I make that same promise? Is it possible to find joy? Every. Single. Day?

Yes! In our walk through this study, we'll begin to recognize reasons to rejoice *every day*! We'll find them in Scripture and in God's truth lived out in our lives . . . on our everyday days and our extraordinary days. On our trying days and our triumphant days. Can I be full of joy each day as the apostle Paul was? (Spoiler alert: Absolutely!)

Although the joy-filled, Spirit-inspired words of Paul were shared first with this faithful Early Church, they quickly became a part of the original canon of Scripture, God's living and active Word for us. God gives us the same encouragement, exhortations, warnings, reassurance, and, above all, good news of His saving grace for us in Christ Jesus. So let's get started!

USING THIS STUDY

The eight weeks of Bible study are divided into five study sessions, forty sessions total. This format is intended to encourage you toward daily devotion time, providing direction for it and joy in it. *Joy* is flexible to be used in personal study or with a group to accommodate ever-changing schedules. Give yourself some grace and enjoy these sessions in a way that works for you.

Here's what you'll find in each session:

☐ **JOY Theme:** "Joy in . . ." Each session title is also its theme, drawn from Philippians. Let God reveal to you, throughout your study and beyond, how you possess this joy.

☐ **Philippians verses:** Each session contains the verses to unpack and apply. You may want to mark, memorize, and journal about these verses throughout this study.

☐ **Reading the Letter:** Examine this portion of Paul's letter in context with other passages in Philippians and across Scripture. Dig in to seek understanding, read stories, respond to questions, and apply all of it to life. As time allows, choose to answer all four daily questions or just one, two, or a few. As you read, alone or with others, *circle what stands out to you*. What really "spoke" to you? You can bring that to the table for group study when each session is reviewed. **I highly recommend you access the answers in the back of the book to the daily questions.**

☐ **Special Delivery:** Here and there is a Special Delivery with information relating to the cultural or historical backdrop or a relevant fact as it applies to the topic of the session.

☐ **JOYFUL Challenge!** Finally, a daily challenge prompts you to apply it *to* or realize it *in* your life. Ask the Lord to show you how to recognize joy and to know with confidence that joy is *yours* every day!

At the end of each week is a **Group Study** overview if you're on this journey with others. Some groups may meet for two-hour weekly study and complete all five study sessions in detail. Some groups meet every other week, or some groups are just two friends joining for mutual accountability and encouragement in God's Word. Whatever your study looks like, *Joy* is complete with these opportunities:

- [ ] **View the optional video segment.** I am overjoyed to join you via video every week to introduce the big picture: topics and themes of Philippians, what makes them applicable, and how to recognize them in your life. You can view or download all eight videos at **cph.org/joy** for no fee.

- [ ] **Review every JOY Theme from this week.** Discuss a favorite question or portion from daily study, along with your answers. Small groups may go around the circle, each participant taking a turn. Large groups may do this table by table.

- [ ] **Talk about your favorite JOYFUL Challenge.**

- [ ] **Share a JOY Snapshot.** See the JOY in God's creation—a sunset, a flower, or a creature. Capture an act of kindness or a smile. Snap a photo of a loved one, event, or familiar place. Thank God for it and let joy flood you. Share your snapshot with your group because *a special scene in the midst of the routine can open our eyes to joy.* **Bonus:** Connect your snapshot with a Bible verse or daily theme, and post it on social media to share your joy even more.

- [ ] **Express JOY!** Unique to each group study is a lively opportunity to express the joy that's yours. Where and how can you express joy, alone and with your group?

- [ ] **Open and close with prayer.** I encourage you to open every study with prayer, asking the Lord to guide and grow you through the Word, by the power of the Holy Spirit. Ask Him to open your heart to the joy He has for you. At the end of the session, let each day's theme and topic serve as a prayer starter. For example, on Day 1, Joy in Believing, you can thank God that you believe, by His grace and through His gift of faith in Christ. Ask Him to help you realize your joy more fully and lead you to share it with others.

Remember, there's no one way or right way to complete *Joy*. May God's guidance lead you to it and His grace carry you through it. Rejoice in the Holy Spirit's work through the Word and in your life today!

> May the God of hope fill you with all joy and peace
> in believing, so that by the power of the Holy Spirit
> you may abound in hope. (**Romans 15:13**)

Joyfully yours in Jesus,
Deb Burma, author

Study Note
Throughout this study, you will see references to other books that informed my writing. Here is a list of abbreviations for the following titles you will see in this study:

CSSB *Concordia Self-Study Bible*

CCBH *Concordia's Complete Bible Handbook*

LBC *Lutheran Bible Companion*

TLSB *The Lutheran Study Bible*

TLDB *Today's Light Devotional Bible*

Joy in Believing

ACTS 16

SHARED HISTORY

When we receive a letter from a loved one, a dear friend, or a close colleague, our quick glance at the sender's name or address reveals a great deal about the letter's contents before we even open the envelope (or the email, text, or message!). How can so little say so much? We have shared history with this person. We know her backstory, and we probably know her heart. We can't wait to receive news, an update, and a good word from her.

Before we "open the envelope" to Paul's Letter to the Philippians, we need to know, as much as possible, what the first recipients would have known as they opened it: the shared history between the sender (Paul) and the recipient (the Church in Philippi); the sender's backstory, purpose, and heart.

A BRIEF BACKDROP

Before we open the Letter of Joy, let's begin by peeking into a few pages of Acts. This New Testament book chronicles the formation and expansion of the Early Church, primarily through the apostles (thus the book title: the Acts of the Apostles), and includes accounts of Paul's missionary journeys.

Led by the Holy Spirit to bring the saving message of Christ beyond Asia Minor and into Macedonia (modern-day Europe) on his second missionary journey, Paul and his companions came first to a leading city of trade, the thriving Roman colony of Philippi (recorded in **Acts 16**). Peeking into this part of his journey will reveal how Paul's ministry and relationship began with the believers in Philippi. We'll understand their close connections and the reasons he rejoices throughout his letter to them.

Special Delivery

A former Pharisee (Jewish religious teacher), Paul had persecuted Christians before Jesus called him to faith and chose him to bring His Good News of salvation to both Jews and Gentiles. Paul shares a brief autobiography in **Acts 26:2–23** for further study into his previous life. We'll learn a lot more about Paul as we go.

As time permits, read **Acts 16:9–24.**

BEGINNINGS . . .

Paul's usual custom upon his arrival in a city was to preach and teach in the city's synagogue. We can surmise that there were too few Jews in Philippi to warrant a synagogue because Paul went outside the city gates, supposing there would be a place of prayer there, near the Gangites River (*CCBH*, p. 376). As Paul shared the saving news of Jesus, a God-fearing businesswoman named Lydia came to faith. Considered the first known convert in Europe, this wealthy seller of purple linens and her family were baptized the same day. And with that, the first church in Europe began. In response to the saving grace she received, Lydia immediately sought to serve the missionaries by offering her home for them. It was, perhaps, the first headquarters for this newly birthed body of believers (*LBC*; vol. 2, p. 539).

AN UNFAIR ARREST . . . AN UNLIKELY RESPONSE

As Paul and his companions continued to proclaim the Gospel in Philippi, he cast out a demon from a slave girl whose owners were profiting by her predictions through the demon. Furious because of their loss of income, her owners made false accusations against Paul and Silas. Soon crowds and officials were involved, and Paul and Silas were wrongly arrested, stripped of their clothes, beaten, and thrown into prison. (The city's magistrates acted unlawfully; as Roman citizens, Paul and Silas were protected against such actions by law [*LBC*, vol. 2, p. 539].) The jailer placed them in the inner prison, used for added security and for torture, forcing their feet in stocks (*CSSB*, p. 1689). He was given orders to secure them especially well, as would be done for the worst of criminals.

Let's look at the miraculous events that followed, beginning with Paul and Silas's unlikely response to their circumstances. Read **Acts 16:25–34** and make note of several highlights.

1. Under the cover of darkness, a beautiful sound rose from the inner prison, and all the prisoners were listening.

    a. What had Paul and Silas just endured? How did they respond, before and immediately after the earthquake? What does this say about them and what they believed?

    b. Were others impacted by Paul and Silas's response? Who and how?

a. Jail. That they were favored by God.
b. Yes, the jailer believed at once and asked to be saved.

> **Special Delivery**
> Philippi was named after King Philip II of Greece, father of Alexander the Great. It was strategically located along the Egnatian Way, a pivotal roadway connecting Rome with the east (*LBC*, vol. 2, p. 539). In God's perfect timing, the creation and expansion of these roadways further enabled the spread of the Gospel.

> **Special Delivery**
> An archaeological discovery in the ruins of ancient Philippi has revealed the bema, or tribunal, within the marketplace where the city's magistrates sentenced Paul and Silas to be flogged and thrown into prison (*LBC*, vol. 2, p. 811).

> **Special Delivery**
> The jailer drew his sword upon himself when he thought his prisoners had escaped because he knew that the penalty under Roman law was death (*TLSB*, p. 1870).

2. Envision a time you (or a loved one) were treated unfairly. Have you suffered unjustly at the hands of others? Were you hurt by gossip, betrayed by a loved one, or passed over for a promotion? What was your reaction? Did others see your faith despite the trials, or did your reaction reveal only anger? How were others impacted by the incident or by your response?

I would love to think that neither you nor I will face harsh treatment or unjust suffering ever (or again), but it's likely we will. Pray for the unshakable joy of the Lord that IS your strength (**Nehemiah 8:10**), that you may respond like Paul and Silas: calm in the face of chaos, rejoicing in the midst of your suffering, confident of your salvation and God's plan for you. Trust that God may use you as His instrument.

3. "What must I do to be saved?" (**Acts 16:30**). How would you respond if someone asked you this question?

Turn to God, repent and praise the Lord always

The missionaries gained the jailer and his entire family for Christ. They baptized and spoke the Word of the Lord to the entire household, and the jailer responded in faith by the Spirit's power.

4. How did the jailer express his new faith?

He rejoiced at having come to faith in God.

Can you imagine Paul's overwhelming joy as he saw how God used this circumstance for good, to bring even the unlikely to faith? Paul could rejoice, even in persecution, that God chose to use him to win people for Christ.

In the morning, the magistrates ordered the release of Paul and Silas, but Paul wasn't going to leave quietly; he wanted to "[establish] their innocence for the sake of the church in Philippi and its future" (*CSSB*, p. 1689). The city would know that he and Silas had been illegally beaten and jailed, though they were innocent (and Roman citizens, at that). Instead of leaving Philippi immediately as the officials had asked, they went to Lydia's, where the believers were gathered, to encourage and embolden them to carry on in faith. As time permits, finish reading **Acts 16:35–40**.

JOYFUL Challenge: "Believe in the Lord Jesus and you will be saved" (**Acts 16:31**). Do you regularly recognize the joy of Christ that's yours because you believe, by the power of the Holy Spirit? Paul and Silas were filled (and overflowed in praise!) with joy in the Lord, all because of their belief and despite the unjust suffering they were enduring. The jailer rejoiced because of his belief, the gift of God given to him that day.

JOY is a fruit of the Holy Spirit (**Galatians 5:22**). What can you do daily to express the joy you've been given so freely because you believe? By God's grace, you can express the JOY inside, not stifle it. You have been empowered by the Holy Spirit . . . so how can you bear His fruit and share His JOY? Maybe you can bear someone's burden, offer an encouraging word, or share a sincere word of thanks.

Joy in Receiving

PHILIPPIANS 1:1–2

YOU'VE GOT MAIL!

I watch for the mailman, and I check my email and text messages a little more often than I'd like to admit, in the hopes that a personal note will be there. I get so excited to receive mail that I might even do a joy dance!

Special Delivery
Most scholars believe Paul penned Philippians around AD 60, near the end of his two-year imprisonment in Rome, and approximately ten years after his first visit to Philippi (his second missionary journey), when he founded the first church in Europe (AD 49–51). He visited the believers in Philippi on his third missionary journey too (see **Acts 20:6**).

Thanks to the return address on the envelope or the contact name on my screen, I know the identity of the sender before I open my letter with a tear, a touch, or a click. Most letter writers today jump right into a salutation. But Paul is careful to clearly identify himself from the beginning, per the conventional letter format of the time, so there is no misunderstanding concerning authorship. Paul also notes that his associate Timothy is by his side; both are servants of their Savior.

BLACK SEA

MACEDONIA

THRACE

ROME

ITALY

PHILIPPI

AEGEAN SEA

MEDITERRANEAN SEA

READING THE LETTER

Paul and Timothy, servants of Christ Jesus, To all the saints in Christ Jesus who are at Philippi, with the overseers and deacons: Grace to you and peace from God our Father and the Lord Jesus Christ. (**Philippians 1:1–2**)

With joy, Paul begins by identifying his beloved recipients, describing to them who they are in Christ and extending a blessing to them. He calls them *saints*, which means they have been made holy, since they're united with Christ by faith.

Believers in Christ, we, too, are sanctified (made to be saints). We're certainly not perfect on our own, but we are united with Christ by faith and covered in His perfection. He took on our sin at His death and conquered both sin and death at His resurrection; He made us right with God (righteous) by faith. We are set apart for God's purposes as His children, heirs of God and coheirs with Christ (**Romans 8:16–17**). All this, packed into one little word: *saint*. What a beautiful opening and an apt description of the Philippian believers and of you and me.

1. When you write, do you include in your salutation (Dear So-and-So) a heartfelt description of the person to whom you're writing? Let's allow this to be a takeaway from Paul's warm opening words. What word or phrase could you include to remind the recipient of her identity?

THEY'VE GOT MAIL

We just peeked into Paul's first trip to Philippi and learned of the events there. As Paul writes this letter ten years later, it's poignant to imagine Lydia and her family, the jailer and his family, and perhaps other former prisoners to be among the many recipients who first read or listen as the letter is shared.

Imagine the Philippians' joy in receiving the letter itself. News from Paul! They know immediately that he is alive and well. And in the first few words, they receive the reminder of their identity in Christ as saints, followed closely with a pronouncement of God's grace and peace upon them.

There is JOY in receiving. Let me remind you that you, too, have received this letter as your very own, and with it, an immediate reminder of your identity in Christ. You are God's child, a *saint*, made holy in your Savior, Jesus, by faith in Him. As the Holy Spirit spoke through Paul, He continues to speak to you and me today through God's Word. Receive His truth with the expectancy that God has something new for you to learn with joy!

Right away, we receive this blessing: God's grace and peace for us in Christ. His grace (unmerited, undeserved favor) is what led Him to send His Son to the cross for us. His peace comes from knowing our sins are forgiven and we are reconciled with God for eternity. The two really belong hand-in-glove, if you will: we are covered in grace and filled with peace.

2. GRACE. Read **Ephesians 2:8–9** and **Romans 3:23–24**. Through these verses and by definition, what do you learn about grace? Why could the grace of God be considered the greatest of all gifts?

Because through his Grace we are saved. Redeemed.

3. PEACE. Paul also pronounces the peace of God in Christ in his opening words. What's unique about the blessing of peace God gives, and why is it incomparably greater than the "peace" the world offers? (Read **John 14:27**, also noting the context.)

Do not let your hearts be troubled or afraid.

4. Who are the people of grace and peace in your life—those who pronounce both blessings into your life when you need them most?

My sister and my cousin

JOYFUL Challenge: Do you receive with a heart of joy? Do you receive well? Consider grace-filled words in a note or letter. Do you believe them as you receive them? When someone speaks truth into your heart, do you listen and let those words bless you or do you dismiss them because you feel undeserving?

A friend told me that the words and Scripture I'd shared during a devotion spoke so specifically to her current struggle that she was certain God had guided her there to hear them. She knew the joy she felt was straight from God, and she praised Him; then she thanked me. I could have dismissed her words, but I didn't. I embraced her, gave the glory to God, and trusted Him to continue working in her life and situation. Receiving her words gave me joy. I knew that the impact of my words was all God's doing—I was only the vessel through which He worked—just as I know that all joy ultimately comes from Him. I'm still learning to receive well. How about you?

My sister in Christ, trust that God is working through another person's gift to you, whether it's words of blessing reminding you of your identity in Christ (like Paul's) or a tangible gift of love. And you, likewise, bring joy to the gift-giver when you receive it with a heart of joy.

Joy as Partners in the Gospel

PHILIPPIANS 1:3-5

I Need an Emoji for Joy

How might someone clearly communicate the fullness of their feelings, especially if they're unable to communicate those feelings face-to-face? Do they use extra adjectives, action verbs, or a variety of emojis?

I'm often teased that my writing conveys my emotions rather plainly when I underline, use all caps, or add an exclamation point (or two)!! Nevertheless, I believe the words a writer chooses should speak for themselves without added emphasis. (Although I'm certain a smiley face or a winky face will help.) Paul's choice of words throughout his letter emphasize the joy that fills him.

Reading the Letter

> I thank my God in all my remembrance of you, always in every prayer of mine for you all making my prayer with joy, because of your partnership in the gospel from the first day until now. **(Philippians 1:3-5)**

Right away, in his opening words, Paul says he always prays for the believers with JOY! His threefold emphasis is all-encompassing: "*Always* in *every* prayer of mine for you *all* making my prayer with joy" (**v. 4**, emphasis added).

☐ Always = He always prays with a heart full of joy for them.

☐ Every = In all of his prayers for them.

☐ All = Every single one of the believers.

Special Delivery
The *Gospel* (Greek *euangelion*) means "good news" or "message." It is the Good News that God has won forgiveness for us because Jesus Christ fulfilled the Law in our place. He paid the price for our sin and provides eternal life by His grace through faith in Him.

1. Why can he pray for them with overwhelming joy?

Because he had the grace of God.

Paul's heart rejoices over the Philippians' reception of the Gospel and over their faithful work to advance the Gospel—partnering with him to expand the kingdom and sending tangible support to him as well, through their brother Epaphroditus. They have labored with Paul, if even from afar, and God has used this support and their prayers to encourage and strengthen Paul in his labor and in his chains.

PARTNERS IN THE GOSPEL

This "partnership in the Gospel" began on the "first day" (v. 5)—when Paul first brought the Good News to Philippi on his second missionary journey. The partnership has been ongoing; it continues even as he writes these joy-filled words. They have a very special bond in the same and shared purpose. This church has grown to become a vibrant body of believers that influences an entire region for Christ.

> **Special Delivery**
> As a prisoner under house arrest, Paul was still expected to provide for himself (**Acts 28:30**), though he was clearly unable to work to support himself. Paul humbly had to rely on the provision of others for his basic needs.

2. Peek ahead to **Philippians 4:15–16** for more details regarding their tangible gift to Paul (delivered by Epaphroditus, who stayed to meet Paul's needs). Read also **2 Corinthians 8:1–5**. What do you learn about the Philippians' generosity and the extent to which they gave to Paul and to others in need?

They were charitable to Paul.

3. How have you tangibly supported others in ministry? Through financial means, food, special gifts, thank offerings, or even boots-on-the-ground help? Describe how it felt to give in this way and other benefits you saw or experienced.

By giving $.

PRAYER WARRIORS

The Philippians were "prayer warriors" on Paul's behalf. My sister Connie is a beautiful example of a "prayer warrior" in my life and on my behalf. She goes to battle for me in prayer, confidently taking each request forward and regularly interceding for me, even when I don't know it. (Praise God, *He* knows just what I need!) Connie patiently prays behind the scenes of my life and the lives of many others. Faithfully. Daily. Diligently. Often she will tell me, after the fact, the many ways she has held up my family and me during a difficult or trying time when only God knew the details. I'm humbled and wowed at His work through each prayer and through her. This woman of faith (and many more) partner with me in the Gospel in such a special way: through prayer. You can imagine that my prayers for *her* are filled with joy in Jesus.

4.   When you read "I thank my God in all my remembrance of you" (**v. 3**), who comes to mind? Who partners in the Gospel with you? (When you pray for them, you can't help but pray with joy because they support you and walk beside you.)

My sisters and brothers.

JOYFUL Challenge: Choose one of the people who came to mind as you considered who partners with you in the Gospel. Stop and revel in the joy that God is flooding into your life through this person. Looking to Paul's example, how might you honor, acknowledge, or thank him or her? How can you, in turn, prayerfully support, encourage, and help this partner, whether he or she is near or far?

Joy as Partakers of God's Grace

PHILIPPIANS 1 : 6 - 8

NOTES OF ENCOURAGEMENT

Notes of encouragement go a long way toward giving us the boost we need in order to realign our focus on our purpose, to reassure us of God's work in and through us, and to remember who (and whose) we are and how much we are loved. As I embarked upon this adventure, writing the words you're reading now, I received some much-needed notes of encouragement. My remarkable friend Lois said, "Deb, I pray for the outpouring of God's blessings as you write, for courage and energy and perseverance." When I thanked her, she elaborated, "Writing, especially for the Lord, is a joy, but it is hard work; it takes *courage* to even start, tons of spiritual, emotional, and physical *energy*, and huge quantities of *perseverance*. Good thing God's providing all of those, in exactly the quantity you will need each day. Love you, my friend! Let me know when you need encouragement!"

READING THE LETTER

And I am sure of this, that He who began a good work in you will bring it to completion at the day of Jesus Christ. It is right for me to feel this way about you all, because I hold you in my heart, for you are all partakers with me of grace, both in my imprisonment and in the defense and confirmation of the gospel. For God is my witness,

how I yearn for you all with the affection of Christ
Jesus. (Philippians 1:6–8)

In this portion of Paul's note, he shares the best kind of en-couragement, providing just the boost he knew the Philippians needed. He rejoices in God's work in the believers' lives. He re-minds them that it was God alone who began His salvation work in them through His Word and promises, and He will carry it to its completion when Christ returns. And meanwhile, He contin-ues to work in and through the believers, enabling them to fulfill His purpose, all the way to the day of Christ.

Likewise for you and me: God began His salvation work in us through His Means of Grace—when He first worked faith in our hearts by the power of the Holy Spirit, at our Baptism or upon our first reception of His Word by faith. And the Author of our faith *continues* His good work in us, transforming us into the likeness of Christ, continually guiding us and guarding our hearts as we grow in His Word, and keeping us in the one true faith until the day of Jesus' return when we will finally see Him face-to-face.

Paul can say with boldness that it's right for him to feel as he does about the believers in Philippi. *How could he feel any other way?* After all, for many years he has witnessed firsthand their growth and unity in faith, their generous gifts, and their perse-verance in the face of persecution (more on that to come).

SHARING IN THE SAME GIFT

Paul's heart is bursting with joy for these people who have received the same undeserved, unearned favor with God as he has. In 4:3, he lovingly affirms that their "names are in the book of life." While I don't regularly use the word *partaker*, it's the perfect defining word for what Paul describes here: recipient, yes, but more than that. A partaker is a *fellow* recipient, sharing in the same gift with others who receive it too. Side by side, chosen children of God in Christ receive God's grace for salvation, and not even persecution or chains can take away what they share. And there's more! This same grace enables them to further the Gospel. God carries forward not only Paul but all believers, con-tinuing His Gospel-proclaiming good work in all . . . and all the way to its completion at the day of Christ.

PARTNERS WHO PARTAKE

We are equipped to be Partners in the Gospel (PG) *because* we are Partakers of Grace (PG) from God! Look around you. Smile. Rejoice! Your sisters in Christ share a very special bond with you as you hold one another in your hearts; you have the

Special Delivery
Partakers (Greek *sygkoinonos*) means "participants" and "sharers."

same and shared purpose, even as the details and the manner in which you share the Gospel are unique to each of you!

The believers have stood by Paul's side as, in freedom and in chains, he shares the saving love of Jesus; as he has defended and confirmed it to both Jews and Gentiles, proclaiming Christ as the perfect fulfillment of all messianic prophesies, of every promise of God (see **2 Corinthians 1:20**).

God, more than anyone, knows Paul's heart. He knows that Paul loves these people and yearns for them with the same affection that Christ Himself has for all. He misses them intensely and longs to see them again.

Special Delivery
"I hold you in my heart" (**Philippians 1:7**). In the Greek, the heart contains a person's personality, feelings, mind, and will. Paul does more than just hold the believers dear; he "holds" them in such a way that they're almost a part of him, ever on his mind and always in his concerns (Lenski, p. 712).

1. Paul's love imitates Christ's love. Describe this kind of love. (Read **John 15:9–12** and **Ephesians 5:2**.)

   He loved his followers as God loved them Jesus gave his life for us.

2. Describe the love at the heart of PG friendships. How can you enrich friendships with those you "hold in your heart"?

   By loving them like God does.

3. "You make known to me the path of life; in Your presence there is fullness of joy; at Your right hand are pleasures forevermore" (**Psalm 16:11**). This psalm of David is quoted by the apostle Peter in **Acts 2:28**, in the earliest days of the church following Jesus' resurrection and ascension to heaven. What do these prophetic words say about Christ? about our source of joy?

   That He's there guiding us through the chosen path.

GRACE—GOD'S GIFT!

My greatest passion is sharing the message of God's grace in written words and as I walk beside women and exclaim to them that we are *partakers of God's grace*. We desperately need His grace, but we can't earn it, and we certainly don't deserve it. In love, God came to us, full of His life-saving grace for us in Christ. He favors us, forgives us, and fills us with faith, by the Spirit's power. Grace is God's gift to us in Christ, and there's nothing that could bring us greater joy!

One evening at a women's event, I devoted the entire topic to grace. At the end, a young woman courageously spoke up. She admitted through tears that while she knew all about God's grace, until that evening, she had not grasped the extent of His grace *for her*. She had secretly held onto shame, believing that God couldn't possibly continue to love and forgive her because of her past and ongoing struggle to forgive another person. She learned anew that she has been forgiven and freed in Christ, the one who enables her to forgive others. She was filled with joy in His salvation and hope for the future—for eternity. God be praised!

4. The joy we have in our salvation is really at the root of all joy. Author Donna Pyle writes, "Joy resides in moments couched in the safety net of salvation" (p. 194). Consider a moment that has brought you joy. How was that *joy moment* (JM) cradled or "couched" within the greater joy of your salvation?

JOYFUL Challenge: As partakers of God's grace, we have the privilege of providing a much-needed *joy boost* to a sister or brother, the reminder that we're walking side by side as fellow recipients, God working in us! Jot a note of encouragement filled with reassurances and a reminder of who (and whose!) they are and how much they are loved. Use this as an excuse to buy some fun stationery! Or grab a card, a pad of paper, or a sticky note right now and write that note! Make a point to mail, give, or post it this week.

Joy in Abundant Love for One Another

PHILIPPIANS 1:9–11

PRAYER TUCKED INSIDE

I opened a letter-length text from a dear friend and found a prayer nestled in the middle of her words of encouragement and comfort. My friend took my concern straight to God and shared her prayer with me. I was doubly blessed, speaking aloud her words in a prayer of my own and knowing she was praying so specifically for my physical and spiritual needs, all out of love for her Savior and for me.

READING THE LETTER

> And it is my prayer that your love may abound more and more, with knowledge and all discernment, so that you may approve what is excellent, and so be pure and blameless for the day of Christ, filled with the fruit of righteousness that comes through Jesus Christ, to the glory and praise of God. (**Philippians 1:9–11**)

Here we find Paul's prayer, tucked inside His joy-filled letter to the believers. (Remember the premise of Paul's prayer, shared in **verses 3–4**: he *always* thanks God for them, and he *always* prays for *all* of them with joy.)

1. How is Christian love for one another defined in Paul's prayer? (Paul prefaced this prayer by sharing his affection with them [**vv. 7–8**]. His love for them imitates Christ's love for all.)

    Filled with ___kindness___ and ___every kind of perception___

2. Read again the entire prayer, **verses 9–11.** Paul wraps it up with the grace-filled reason their love may abound. Reading **verses 9–10** in light of **verse 11,** explain how Paul's prayer may be realized.

Let's look again at **verse 9.** To "abound" is to have in abundance, right? Synonymous with "overflowing" (*TLSB*, p. 1990), this is the measure of love that Paul prays they have for one another. And not just abounding, but "more and more"—ever-growing. Paul prays that their love continues to increase, as should be the natural direction in the life of every Christian and every church, with God's help. It's no small thing that a measure of JOY results as well.

Love in Knowledge; Knowledge in Love!

Paul doesn't pray their love will grow deeper in feelings; he purposely connects love with knowledge and discernment. Maybe this connection is surprising since we live in a world where love is often limited to a feeling or sentiment. Elsewhere, Paul is careful to note that to have knowledge without love is to be nothing (**1 Corinthians 13:2**). But knowledge belongs to love, and the two shouldn't be separated. "Paul's prayer is, then, that love may abound in its natural, native connection with true knowledge of the heart, . . . this means stronger, wiser, abler love. Love is an active attribute, it reaches *out* and bestows; knowledge and perception bring *into* love what its nature requires for its work" (Lenski, p. 718). To love well—to abound in active love toward others—we first need to be filled with knowledge and insight.

It's through the knowledge and revelation of God's Word that we can even know what love is. God's love is everlasting (**Psalm 103:17**). By very definition of love (Greek *agape*), it is without limits or conditions. His love is wholly sacrificial (**John 3:16**), and nothing can separate us from it (**Romans 8:39**). God IS love (**1 John 4:8**), and we're able to love one another because He first loved us (**1 John 4:19**).

I continually stand in amazement of God's boundless love, at His miraculous work through His Word, enabling you and me to receive by faith the *knowledge* of this and all truth. Love informed by knowledge of the truth enables a believer to then discern what is best—to "approve what is excellent." To be discerning is to test everything to Scripture, to recognize what has value. By the Spirit's power, we also discern right from wrong, divine truth from "religious" lies, good from evil, and that which is according to the Word versus that which stands in opposition to the Word.

Special Delivery
While there are four Greek words for our one English word for love, *agape* is the Greek word used to define God's undeserved, perfect love for us that is both self-giving and sacrificial. This is the kind of love we're to have for one another (*LBC*, vol. 2, p. 924).

3. Read **1 Thessalonians 3:12** and **Colossians 1:9**. In these letters, too, Paul talks about love and knowledge. In your own words and based upon these passages, share what you know about God's desires for us and His work in us.

Through prayer obtain more understanding of God's Word.

COMPLEMENTS!

Love and knowledge *complement* each other. Consider your relationships with others and how love deepens as you grow to know one another more intimately—sharing your heart, interests, thoughts, and priorities. Love increases as knowledge grows. Now consider how much greater this same principle is in your relationship with the Lord. Learn the depth of His love (although you and I cannot fully grasp the limitless depth of God's love for us) and grow in your love for Him and your knowledge of His will as you walk in His Word. There, you see His heart for you in Christ, His thoughts of you, and His promises for you. His ways are excellent; His plans are best.

4. Consider these two questions about love and knowledge.

   a. What's so important about being able to "approve what is excellent" (**Philippians 1:10**) or discern what is best? How does this impact our love for one another?

   It becomes more clear and greater.

   b. By the fruit produced in us (all we think, say, and do), we desire to live righteous lives in Christ. What's the ultimate purpose of life lived by His righteousness? Does "pure and blameless" mean without sin (**v. 10**)?

   Yes

JOYFUL Challenge: Abundant love. In response to this gift, received in Christ and growing toward others as you grow in God's Word, how can you live out *abundant love* today? Express it in words. Use Paul's prayer here to guide your own prayer letter to someone special—a PG friend: a Partaker of Grace who Partners in the Gospel with you. Remember, too, Paul's premise (**1:3–4**) and his preface (**1:7–8**) as you consider what you'd like to say. (Write it out, type it, or text it ... however you express it, make sure you send it.) And you can sign it *"Joyfully yours."*

Week 1
Group Study

- ☐ **Review every JOY theme from this week.**

- ☐ **Take turns sharing a portion or favorite question,** along with your answers, from each study session, and discuss.

  1. Joy in Believing

  2. Joy in Receiving

  3. Joy as Partners in the Gospel

  4. Joy as Partakers of God's Grace

  5. Joy in Abundant Love for One Another

- ☐ **Talk about Your Favorite JOYFUL Challenge.**

- ☐ **Share a JOY Snapshot.** (See a general description in the Introduction, page 9.)

Express JOY!

You've heard of a "happy dance," right? It's a fun little boogie reserved for those moments when something so outrageously good, exciting, or earth-shattering happens that we simply must get up and dance! I have news for you: because joy is ours always, not contingent upon our circumstances and certainly not reserved for mountaintop moments alone, you and I can JOY DANCE any ole' time. Like now! Go ahead and get up . . . show others your best moves. Okay, so maybe you don't dance, at least not in front of anyone but the woman in the mirror. Tap your toes where you are; move your shoulders, wave your hands, and bob your head.

In 2 Samuel, you can read that King David "danced before the Lord with all his might" as he rejoiced in God's presence (**6:14**). And *you* can rejoice as you share the words of the psalmist: "Praise His name with dancing" (**Psalm 149:3**). Express the joy that cannot be contained: Jesus is risen, and you *believe*. By faith, you have *received*. You *partner* in the Gospel and *partake* of God's grace. And you *overflow* in love for one another, just as God's love overflows for YOU! Soooo . . . if you're feeling spontaneous (or merely challenged by the women in your midst), give it a whirl (literally). Tell the Lord, "I am joyfully Yours, Jesus!"

Joy in Seeing God's Hand

PHILIPPIANS 1:12-13

PERSONAL NEWS

When the wife of a deployed soldier learned about a skirmish where her husband was serving, she waited with bated breath for news from him. And the letter that followed was like pure gold in her hands as she read, in his own handwriting, his personal news that he was safe. Alive. Well. And bravely continuing to serve with joy for the sake of every soldier around him and every civilian back home, knowing that God's hand continued to rest upon him in his service.

A letter sharing personal news feels like a warm hug. It's a relief to learn that our loved one is alive and well. Personal news puts us "there" with them as we envision them in their current circumstances and know more about how we can pray for and support them.

READING THE LETTER

I want you to know, brothers, that what has happened to me has really served to advance the gospel, so that it has become known throughout the whole imperial guard and to all the rest that my imprisonment is for Christ. (**Philippians 1:12–13**)

Paul's brothers and sisters in Philippi know his current circumstance in some detail already. They know when he says "what has happened to me" that he is speaking of his current imprisonment. Paul addresses the concern he knows the believers have for him.

The earliest Philippian believers who had witnessed the events recorded in **Acts 16** had likely told of those events to the newcomers of the growing church. So the recipients of this letter had either seen firsthand or heard secondhand of Paul's joyful demeanor, actions, and response in the face of persecution in Philippi.

Under House Arrest, Advancing the Gospel

At the writing of this letter, Paul is detained under house arrest, so he's not in a dungeon, but still under constant guard, and likely chained to a soldier. He's nearing the end of a two-year wait for a trial, and friends are permitted to visit and attend to his needs. "He lived there two whole years at his own expense, and welcomed all who came to him, proclaiming the kingdom of God and teaching about the Lord Jesus Christ with all boldness and without hindrance" (**Acts 28:30–31**).

> **Special Delivery**
> "Whole imperial guard" = a contingent of soldiers numbering several thousand (*CSSB*, p. 1816), assigned to specific tasks for the emperor, senators, or other officials of the government (*TLSB*, p. 2032).

1. What words come to mind to describe Paul's circumstances? Is he sulking, trembling, fretting, or grumbling? (Would you be?)

2. What's one major way this imprisonment has "served to advance the gospel" (**Philippians 1:12**)? (Paul lists two major ways. Today we'll look at the first.)

Clearly, Paul has been quite a witness in Rome. He recognizes his influence among the many guards who have been assigned individually to a rotated watch over him; since Paul includes the *entire* imperial guard, we know that his message has spread even further among them.

Paul has taken every opportunity to share salvation in Jesus with every person in his midst. In his "defense and confirmation of the gospel"—the hearing of Paul's appeal to Caesar—the Gospel of Christ has come before "the supreme court of the world" (Lenski, p. 725). And far beyond the courtroom, the Good News has been heard by "all the rest." This means news has spread all across Rome, from the lowliest in the general population to all in Caesar's palace to the powerful Roman military. No wonder Paul is rejoicing!

3. Read **2 Timothy 2:9**, where Paul writes to Timothy regarding a later imprisonment. Why is he bound here? But what is not bound?

While we might look at this time of imprisonment and think, "What a waste of Paul's time," time is never wasted in God's economy. Paul trusts God's timing and has accepted his own physical limitations, trusting the Lord to work mightily *in* them, *through* them, and *beyond* them. Consider the time it sometimes takes to establish relationship and trust, to gain a willing ear to listen. Paul's winsome attitude and joy-filled demeanor would have won over soldiers, civil and religious leaders, and others who served the authorities in Rome. I can almost envision each soldier vying for his turn to guard Paul.

Can you see how God has been using Paul's circumstances for good? Paul does. Though he includes personal news, he barely addresses how he is doing; instead, he selflessly emphasizes that his imprisonment has served to advance the Gospel. This is always Paul's primary concern, and what a reason to rejoice!

> **Special Delivery**
> Paul doesn't say how many souls have been won for Christ, only that he has done what he has been called to do by sharing the Gospel "with all boldness and without hindrance" (**Acts 28:31**). Paul leaves the rest to God. (See also **1 Corinthians 3:6–9**.)

4. Recall the words you chose to describe Paul's circumstances. (Words like uncertain, lonely, unbearable, unjust, persecuted, mistreated.) Could you at times relate some of these words to your life? What holds you prisoner? What can help you hang on?

LIMITATIONS

Perhaps you haven't been treated unjustly or persecuted for sharing the love of your Savior, but you have experienced physical or geographic restrictions, financial or circumstantial constraints. Limitations that keep you from thinking you can make a difference or have an impact on others.

How might God use you, within your limitations, to do "far more abundantly than all that [you] ask or think, according to the power at work within [you]" (**Ephesians 3:20**)?

OUR WITNESS IN TIMES OF STRUGGLE AND SUFFERING

Times of struggle are opportunities to witness Christ to others. How we respond to struggles in front of a watching world says much about our faith and even more about the God we serve. During difficult times, it's hard to praise God—but that's His desire and His *will* for us: "Rejoice always, . . . give thanks in all circumstances, for this is the will of God in Christ Jesus for you" (**1 Thessalonians 5:16, 18**). Our response, by God's grace, can speak volumes to everyone around us, put a spring in our own step, and gain a listening ear.

My friend Kris suffered with debilitating back pain and learned that surgery was imminent. Although she was afraid, she humbly admitted her fears and courageously asked for prayers from friends and family members. Kris saw her pain and the process—surgery to recovery and therapy—as opportunities to praise her Lord for His answers to those prayers. She saw her situations as a chance to witness to her surgeon (whom she asked to join her family in prayer) and many on the medical staff. She boldly shared one blessing after another, recognizing each as coming straight from the hand of God, her ever-present help in trouble (**Psalm 46:1**). Kris knows that sometimes blessings come in at-first-unrecognizable packages, but oh, the unspeakable joy when they're opened and celebrated!

JOYFUL Challenge: Paul shares what I call a "Joy Moment" (JM) as, in the midst of imprisonment, he sees how God is using his difficult circumstance for a purpose. Maybe we won't recognize a JM until later; maybe we will be unable to see a purpose for our pain until the day of Jesus' return. Maybe a JM will jump out at us, while others may be more subtle, to be searched out when our eyes are open to see them. Obvious or subtle, JMs should be noted, shared, and even celebrated (what a witness, when they are!). We can think about them on difficult days that dull our awareness of the joy that is ours. JM reminders show us and others a God who is greater than our circumstances.

Recall a specific circumstance when you could see God's hand, either during it or as you looked back, as He used it for good. For His purpose. For a witness of Christ's love to another. (Read **Romans 8:28** aloud.) Ask for eyes wide open to spot a JM and note it! Share it! Celebrate it! Jot it in your Bible or in a journal. Tuck it away so you can pull it out when you (or someone else) need it most.

Joy in Seeing Others Proclaim Jesus

PHILIPPIANS 1:14-18A

A Missionary on the Go

My friend Sarah is a medical missionary in East Africa. I wait for her newsletter every month, and I joy dance when I receive a warm note directly from her. While her news-filled letters contain updates about herself, they're centered on the Gospel work God is doing through the many missionaries and other believers who've been emboldened by Sarah and others. She humbly and gladly shares the efforts of every courageous short-term mission team and asks for prayer as they partner in the Gospel with her in varying ways—*speaking the Word without fear*. Sarah is always on the go, sometimes visiting distant villages to provide medical care and the love of Jesus; but others may be able to go where Sarah cannot. She trains and teaches those who have the means to reach people beyond her geographic limitations.

Reading the Letter

And most of the brothers, having become confident in the Lord by my imprisonment, are much more bold to speak the word without fear. Some indeed preach Christ from envy and rivalry, but others from good will. The latter do it out of love, knowing that I am put here for the defense of the gospel. The former proclaim Christ out of selfish ambition, not sincerely but thinking to afflict me in my imprisonment. What then? Only that in every way, whether in pretense or in truth, Christ is proclaimed, and in that I rejoice. (**Philippians 1:14–18a**)

Paul has been a man on the go for Jesus, passionately spreading the Gospel, journeying far and wide to begin churches, sharing Christ with both Jews and Gentiles. Imagine the sudden and long-term halt this detainment brought, confining Paul to a small space, chained to a soldier. Paul would be justified if he were restless and frustrated, but he sees beyond his forced limitations. The Gospel is in no way confined, but is spreading greatly through others who respond to Paul's faith. Amazing, right? Paul's detention has not hindered the Gospel—it has *served to make it known* in yet another major way.

EMBOLDENED!

In the midst of and even as a result of Paul's suffering, other Christians (brothers) in Rome are emboldened to "speak the word without fear" (**v. 14**). They know the real reason Paul is imprisoned, and they want to take the same bold stance for Christ he has taken (*CSSB*, p. 1817). More believers than ever are courageously proclaiming the Word of God, fearlessly sharing their faith. God uses Paul to inspire them. They are emboldened to step up and do what Paul cannot. His joy and passion for sharing the Gospel are contagious.

1. Paul's circumstances inspired differing reactions among the believers in Rome who are sharing the Gospel. Both camps are emboldened, but their motives are divergent. Describe the two motives, based on the details we're given in **verses 15–17**.

2. Although some preach with jealousy or selfish motives, why does Paul still *rejoice*?

Christ is *still* preached! Lost and hurting souls are *still* being reached with the Good News of Jesus! "Those who preach with wrong, insincere motives do so out of a sense of competition with Paul and so think they are making his imprisonment more difficult to bear" (*CSSB*, p. 1817). But even those who preach with wrong motives are still preaching *Christ*; they're not heretics, not false teachers (Lenski, p. 729) (see Special Delivery). Here, the brothers' message is pure, even if their motives are not, and God will use the pure proclamation of His Word to instill faith in human hearts. The Gospel is advanced—and that is reason to rejoice.

Special Delivery
False teachers and false gospels pose a threat, then and now. When the pure message of Christ is tainted, undermined, added to, or taken away from, it's no longer the Gospel (see **Galatians 1:6–9**). Selfish motives cannot be confused with corrupted teachings. Paul adamantly warns against false teachers and gospels, as we'll explore more in chapter 3.

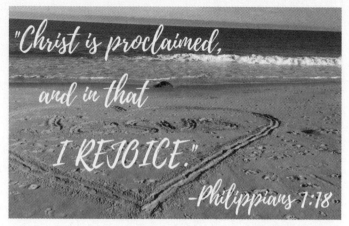

"Christ is proclaimed, and in that I rejoice" (**Philippians 1:18**). My friend and I proclaimed Jesus on the beach, creating this giant heart containing His name. We hoped hotel guests would gaze upon the heart and long to learn more or become emboldened themselves to proclaim His name. (We saw a few taking photos!)

3. When have you struggled to rejoice over someone's message, though the content was pure, because you doubted their motives were pure? (No names, please). What lessons could we take from Paul here? What might help us have a change of heart?

4. How does Paul's attitude and response differ toward those who want to honor Paul and proclaim Christ out of love, and those who see the chance to win influence for themselves and proclaim Christ out of envy? **Verse 18** begins "What then?" What does Paul mean by this?

PURE PROCLAMATION!

Our twins' kindergarten teacher, Mrs. Stange, called one evening to report a special moment. During devotion time, she was talking about all the bad things we say and do. "That's called sin. And we all sin, don't we?" she confessed. One little boy shot up his hand, begging to speak. "Nuh-uh, Mrs. Stange," he challenged. "Courtney doesn't sin. She doesn't do anything wrong!" My daughter gasped. "I do too! I sin all the time!" she shot back. (Courtney was a timid student, so her bold response *and* what followed took everyone by surprise.) Mrs. Stange sat back and let Courtney take the floor. My daughter continued her declaration, sharing everyone's need for a Savior and Jesus' perfect provision (in kindergarten language, of course). Mrs. Stange shared her JOY in seeing someone else proclaim the saving love of Jesus, with the simple motive of making certain everyone knew the truth.

Could we say the same of our motives? If we're honest, we would admit that sometimes we're more concerned about receiving admiration from others than we are about the heart of the matter. Other times we're afraid to take a stand for the truth. Ouch! Like Courtney said, we sin all the time and desperately need a Savior. Thank You, Jesus, for Your perfect fulfillment of our every need. For Your forgiveness. For faith that enables us to be motivated only by love in our response to others and our declaration of the Gospel.

JOYFUL Challenge: Name some Christ-followers who have influenced you to go and do likewise. Maybe they are quiet workers, serving selflessly behind the scenes for their Savior, unnoticed by others. Maybe they're faithful witnesses of Christ in the workplace, gently sharing their faith with their words and choices. Maybe they head committees, lead children, serve in the mission field, teach adults, or sing praises in a band. Maybe they've even nurtured you. What encouraged or emboldened you most by their influence upon you? Today, choose one of these people of influence and reach out to him or her. Let this impactful person know that it brought you JOY to see them proclaim Jesus. Share how you've been inspired to live your witness in your own way. Write a letter, send a text, make a phone call, or give a gift—and thank Jesus for them as you do!

Joy in Answered Prayer and the Spirit's Help

PHILIPPIANS 1:18B-19

WORDS OF JOY AMID WINDS OF UNCERTAINTY

As I pen these words to you, I have a dear friend who is holding up under some fierce winds of change. She's learning to go with the f-l-o-w while at the same time staying the course. She recognizes that the Lord is both holding her firmly *and* carrying her along, amid the wild winds. And few friends recognize JOY in the midst of wild-winded change and uncertainty quite like she does, as evidenced in her regular cards and texts.

She knows that I'm writing to YOU about joy, and she has kept this three-letter word in the forefront of her thoughts. While she doesn't know what's coming next, she is able, by God's grace, to know that *the joy of the Lord is her strength*. And she takes time to communicate her joy to me: "I don't have to know the future outcome of this uncertain time, but I can trust God, live in the present . . . and recognize the joys I'm blessed with each day." Yes, that's my friend, staying the course in her Savior's strength.

READING THE LETTER

Yes, and I will rejoice, for I know that through your prayers and the help of the Spirit of Jesus Christ this will turn out for my deliverance. (**Philippians 1:18b–19**)

It's difficult to pen words of JOY to a loved one when the future (or the present) is uncertain. Then how is it that Paul can write with such joy, even as he doesn't know if he will soon be released, further detained, or even executed? I think we know the answer already! And Paul gives credit where credit is due, with the help of the Spirit of Jesus Christ.

Yesterday, we read that Paul is rejoicing over the continued expansion of God's kingdom as others proclaim Jesus (**v. 18a**). Now, in the second half of the same verse, he says "rejoice" again. He is already rejoicing—for good reason. And now, for yet another reason, he says he *will* rejoice.

1. "Yes, and I will rejoice" (**v. 18b**).

   a. What's another reason Paul will rejoice in "this"—his current and anticipated circumstances (not just his imprisonment, but the impending trial and subsequent outcome of his appeal to Caesar)—his defense and confirmation of the Gospel? With what words do we know Paul is confident of this outcome?

   b. Through what two things is he certain that his circumstances will end with his deliverance? How are they connected?

THE PRIVILEGE TO PRAY

One of the most important ways we help, support, and walk beside other believers—our partners in the Gospel—is in our prayers for them. What a privilege it is to pray! We have an almighty God who hears and answers every single one. Besides those closest to you, who else can you support in this vital mission and how?

☐ Pray for those who are taking risks as they courageously share Jesus at home and across the world:

☐ Pray for their physical and spiritual protection.

☐ Pray that they may stand firm, not caving to a wayward culture or backing down when ridiculed or opposed.

☐ Pray that they may continue to share fearlessly!

☐ Pray for the Spirit's strength, counsel, and comfort over them.

The Helper

Paul is confident that the Holy Spirit will give him strength, courage, and words as he appeals to Caesar; as he defends and confirms the Gospel, for which he is on trial. The "Spirit of truth," the "Helper," will testify about Jesus through Paul. (See **John 15:26**.)

2. Jesus forewarned His followers that they would be persecuted for His sake. How does Jesus comfort and prepare them in **Matthew 10:18–20** and **Luke 12:11–12**? How will they be helped?

Deliverance

What a beautiful word: *deliverance!* To be delivered from something is to be saved or spared. When God called Moses, it was for the deliverance of His people from captivity (**Exodus 6:1–8**). David rejoiced in praise to God, who had delivered him from the hand of King Saul and from the hands of his enemies (**2 Samuel 22:1**). Countless times, as God's people and prophets cried out in their distress or persecution, God heard their prayers and delivered them, according to His will. So we read Paul's word *deliverance* and think, "Paul is certain of an upcoming release, and that means he will go on living." But as we look ahead, we see Paul rejoices in a much richer deliverance.

Special Delivery
"The Spirit of Jesus Christ." The Holy Spirit is not only the Spirit of God the Father but also of God the Son (see **Romans 8:9**). The Spirit is sent by the Father *and* by the Son (see **John 14:16–17**; **Galatians 4:6**; *CSSB*, p. 1817).

3. How can Paul say he is certain this will turn out for his deliverance, no matter the outcome? What is Paul's richer understanding of this beautiful word? How does this apply to us?

Jesus, our Savior, "who was delivered up for our trespasses and raised for our justification" (**Romans 4:25**), delivered us from a fate far worse than a two-year detainment or even life imprisonment; He delivered us from the captivity and slavery of our sin, from eternal death and separation from God.

4. According to **Galatians 1:4**; **Colossians 1:13**; and **1 Thessalonians 1:10**, from what has Jesus delivered us by His death and resurrection?

JOYFUL Challenge: *Joy in Answered Prayer:* God hears and answers every prayer offered in Jesus' name by faith, but too often we don't recognize His answer, we take it for granted, or we fail to see it entirely. Out of His love for you, He is faithful to answer, according to His will and in His perfect timing. Recall one specific time when prayer was answered in such a way that you could not miss it. Rejoice in your remembrance of God's perfect provision, deliverance, or protection through answered prayer.

Joy in the Spirit's Help: Can you recall a time you asked God to give you the words to say, and later you were humbled by someone's response, that your faith-filled words provided just what they needed? You have hidden His Word in your heart and requested wisdom and strength. You've asked for His help and earnestly sought to speak His truth into each situation. You may find yourself thinking, "Did I say that?" While you may not remember, you can trust the Holy Spirit's work through you—for the good of someone else and all for His glory. Rejoice!

Joy No Matter What!

PHILIPPIANS 1:20-26

HOPES AND EXPECTATIONS

Forthright. Gut-level honesty, vulnerable and real. When a friend shares her thoughts this way, when she reveals her desires and struggles, and especially as they pertain to her concern for you, know that you are blessed with the richest kind of friendship. She knows you so well. She can write to you from deep within her heart, sharing the hopes and expectations she has. Often, it takes time and years to develop this kind of friendship and this level of communication.

READING THE LETTER

As it is my eager expectation and hope that I will not be at all ashamed, but that with full courage now as always Christ will be honored in my body, whether by life or by death. For to me to live is Christ, and to die is gain. If I am to live in the flesh, that means fruitful labor for me. Yet which I shall choose I cannot tell. I am hard pressed between the two. My desire is to depart and be with Christ, for that is far better. But to remain in the flesh is more necessary on your account. Convinced of this, I know that I will remain and continue with you all, for your progress and joy in the faith, so that in me you may have ample cause to glory in Christ Jesus, because of my coming to you again. (**Philippians 1:20–26**)

Paul enjoys depth in his relationship with the believers in Philippi, and in these verses he expresses his deepest desire and his struggles, especially as they relate to them, his dear friends, who've partnered in the Gospel with Paul for years. He has confident *hope* in his Savior (not "wishful thinking" as we often define hope) and *eager expectation* that with the Spirit's help he will maintain courage and honor his Savior, in life and in death. (Paul's long-term imprisonment and suffering could tempt him to "abandon ship" or to weaken his resolve, bringing shame upon himself and hurting the cause of the Gospel.) The Spirit will enable Paul to speak with courage and boldness.

Paul knows he's been called by God according to His purpose, and he knows, by faith, that "all things work together for good" (**Romans 8:28**). It's as if he is saying, "No matter what happens, I'll be okay because I know my Savior will deliver me."

1. "To live is _____, and to die is _____" (**Philippians 1:21**). In your own words, share what you think each one-word possibility means for Paul and for us.

Paul's JOY is in Christ. All of life's meaning is found in Him. To go on living means advancing Christ's Gospel; to live for His purposes. To die is to be with Christ eternally—even better! "Here Paul is saying that his ultimate concern and most precious possession, both now and forever, is Christ and his relationship to him" (*CSSB*, p. 1817).

"To Depart and Be with Christ"

This short phrase has so much significance. "While mysteries remain, this passage clearly teaches that when believers die they are with Christ, apart from the body" (*CSSB*, p. 1817). For a person of faith, to depart by death IS to be with Christ. "[This] is the assured hope of every dying Christian . . . the soul is with Christ, glorious, in bliss" (Lenski, p. 747). Paul knows, too, that at the day of Christ, he will join all believers in the final resurrection.

Hard Pressed

Paul is hard pressed between departing to be with Christ and remaining in the flesh. These are conflicting desires that we face too, aren't they? As God's children, we're passionate about helping those around us; after all, we're "created in Christ Jesus for good works, which God prepared beforehand, that we should walk in them" (**Ephesians 2:10**). At the same time, we wait anxiously for the day when we'll be perfected in Christ, fully reunited with our Savior (see **1 Corinthians 13:12**). Our hope of eternal life makes us all the more anxious to share Jesus' saving love with as many people as possible so they can live with the same certainty. *One inspires the other!* "When Paul says he is 'hard pressed' between the two, he is talking about the power of the significance of each place upon his life, not his intent or ability to choose. Though Paul expresses the question of what he shall choose, he knows that the choice is not his" (Eschelbach, pp. 601–2).

2. How do Paul's desires take a back seat to the believers, for their "progress and joy in the faith" (**Philippians 1:25**)? If Paul remains, what other wonderful thing will result?

Special Delivery
Paul was, in fact, released. He lived to proclaim Jesus' saving love for a few more years before he faced his final imprisonment. See **2 Timothy 4:6**, where Paul says, "The time of my departure has come." In AD 68, the Roman emperor Nero ordered Paul's execution (*LBC*, vol. 2, p. 412).

Paul keeps his head about him, calmly sharing possible outcomes. He may be executed; he may be exiled, or—as he is optimistic—he may be released. His life is in God's hands, and he writes with confidence and joy; he seeks to instill the same in the hearts of every reader.

TIMES OF STRUGGLE

In times of struggle, our ultimate JOY is found in the hope we have in Jesus Christ, so we ask for eyes to see beyond the here-and-now, peering ahead to the eternal life we'll have with Him. My friend and fellow author Jessica Bordeleau wrote, "The Christian life is not some great game of make-believe. Our Christian witness does not require that we fake cheerfulness and paste a false smile on our faces. It's okay to acknowledge the times of struggle and difficulty. We can feel miserable in grief or pain but still draw strength from the inner joy that is God's gift to us in Christ" (*5 Meaningful Minutes for Moms*, pp. 9–10).

3. Without a doubt, this is a time of struggle and difficulty for Paul; he lives with real uncertainty whether he will live or die. Maybe you're going through a struggle (although it is probably vastly different from Paul's). In your far-from-make-believe life, you won't always smile. But what promise can you cling to in the midst of every difficulty? Take another look at **Romans 8:28** and write it here:

4. Can you see how God might use your difficult circumstances for good? for His purpose? to advance the Gospel? Journal your thoughts. Pray for the ability to draw strength from the ultimate joy that's yours because of God's gift to you in Christ.

My Challenge: No Matter What

One day, I was challenged to answer these questions:

☐ Can you say, as Paul did, that no matter what happens, you will be okay? "To live is Christ, and to die is gain" (**Philippians 1:21**).

☐ What does "fruitful labor" mean for you?

After some soul searching, I wrote, "Yes, I believe that no matter what happens to me, I'm gonna be okay because my Savior will deliver me. In fact, I can *rejoice*! If I'm to die for my faith, it IS greater by far because I'll be delivered into the arms of Jesus. I don't have to fear death; I can rest in knowing that when my tasks here are complete, He will bring me home. I trust that God has meaningful work for me to do. So I pray to look at each day with eager anticipation that God will lead my labor for the good of someone else, to proclaim Him through my words, in my interactions, and throughout my life. May He who lives *in* me also work *through* me so Christ is honored and glorified in all I say and do."

JOYFUL Challenge: Now it's your turn! I challenge you to answer the questions that were asked of me: Can you say, as Paul did, that no matter what happens, you will be okay? That "to live is Christ, and to die is gain" (**1:21**)? Pray about it. Talk about it (or write a letter) to a trusted friend. What meaningful work does God have for you? How can you face each day with eager anticipation?

Joy in Unity and in Suffering

PHILIPPIANS 1:27-30

STAND STRONG, SIDE BY SIDE

I recently exchanged a series of emails with a dear friend. A God-fearing matriarch in a small, remote Canadian village, she and her family have welcomed our church's mission team for thirteen consecutive summers, and we were reunited when I returned last summer.

Her message began, "Need prayers for our community. So much is going wrong. I had a prayer group one night here. It was so beautiful. . . . I hang on to Jesus and His Word, and I thank you all for coming every year. You don't realize the hope and strength you give to us, sharing your love of God. It's a courage we all need, to keep moving forward. We get laughed at and made fun of, but my belief is strong that He stands beside us!"

I replied, "I am so touched to know you held a time of prayer and that there are others beside you, trusting in Jesus! Keep standing strong in your faith walk, not worried about anyone laughing or making fun of you, but pressing on, knowing that you have hope and you are not giving up on the people around you, whom you love!"

I couldn't help but think of the believers in Philippi as I wrote to her, encouraging her and all the believers by God's grace to stand strong in the faith despite their suffering.

READING THE LETTER

Only let your manner of life be worthy of the gospel of Christ, so that whether I come and see you or am absent, I may hear of you that you are standing firm in one spirit, with one mind striving side by side for the faith of the gospel, and not frightened in anything by your opponents. This is a clear sign to them of their destruction, but of your salvation, and that from God. For it has been granted to you that for the sake of Christ you should not only believe in Him but also suffer for His sake, engaged in the same conflict that you saw I had and now hear that I still have. (**Philippians 1:27–30**)

Paul encourages the believers to conduct themselves in a manner worthy of—consistent with—the Gospel of Christ. Their words and actions should reflect the influence the Gospel has on them, by the Spirit's power. Their lives are to mirror God's saving work in them by Christ: loving as He loves and living upright lives with obedience and integrity. "Christ's heroic efforts on their behalf allow them to enjoy a manner of life worthy of His Gospel" (*TLSB*, p. 2029).

Paul yearns to see them and is optimistic that he will (remember **verse 26**: he's hopeful he will come to them again). Whether he is with them face-to-face or only receives reports, he is confident their lives are reflecting the Gospel's work in them, and he builds on this, calling them to the same thing to which Christians are called today.

1. Fill in each word from **Philippians 1:27–30**:

Stand firm in one _____ = Christians defend the Gospel as *one* in the Lord, not compromising truth; all are filled with the same Spirit of Christ. It's by the Spirit's power through God's Word that all of this is possible.

_____ side by side (**with one mind**) = UNITY. Especially when the Gospel is under attack, Christians must link arms and defend the truth, unified with single-mindedness, passion, and purpose. "Paul knew that divisiveness in the Philippian congregation would weaken its ability to persevere in the face of opposition" (Gernant Dumit, p. 17).

Special Delivery

"Striving side by side for the faith of the gospel" (**v. 27**). We may be tempted to believe "striving" here means trying our hardest to believe, as if we attain faith by our efforts or decision. On the contrary, the Gospel produces faith; we receive it by the power of the Holy Spirit. We are saved not by works, but by grace alone through faith alone (**Ephesians 2:8–9**). In *response*, we strive with fellow believers to spread the saving love of Jesus.

Not frightened . . . by your _____ = Standing together as one, Christians don't need to fear opposition, insults, or persecution. In fact, they can be joyfully courageous. After all, "if God is for us, who can be against us?" (**Romans 8:31**).

Special Delivery
Who were these opponents in Philippi? While some think they were hostile Jews, there were only a few Jews in the city, and even Paul's conflict there had not been with them. These opponents were pagan and the kind and scope of opposition that could move the city authorities to action (judging from **v. 30**) (Lenski, p. 755).

2. What difficult message does Paul give (**vv. 28–30**)? What words and phrases reveal what the believers are facing?

FEARLESS!

During a childhood family vacation in the Black Hills of South Dakota, my little sister, Lisa, and I went for a walk in the woods. She was not an average six-year-old; a degenerative epileptic disease necessitated medication that energized her, to say the least. Add to that the fact that she appeared to have no fears. Imagine what ensued when a big, black snarling dog charged in our direction. I screamed, "Help! Someone, help!" as I beckoned Lisa to follow me, turned tail, and ran (as if nine-year-old me could outrun this dog). Lisa, instead, ran straight toward the dog at full speed, fearless. I surmise that because he sensed no fear in her, he literally TURNED TAIL and ran away. She didn't realize she had taken a risk; he could have attacked, but her bravery and love compelled her forward. My little hero taught me a lot that day.

When we consider those who oppose or attack us because we represent Christ, we don't need to run away. In His strength, we can face opposition head-on, standing firm in our faith, so unified that we contend as if we are one. We can take courage in the power of His might. We can do more than just defend our ground; we can move straight toward opposition at full speed, fearless, sharing the Gospel in love.

REJOICE IN SUFFERING?

Paul says the believers' suffering has been given to them as a gift or a privilege, even graciously "granted to" them.

3. How did the apostles Peter and John respond to the persecution they had just endured, recorded in **Acts 5** (see **v. 41**)? What do Peter and James, respectively, have to say about how we can respond in suffering and trials: **1 Peter 4:13–14** and **James 1:2–4**?

What a privilege and an honor to suffer for the sake of the Gospel, knowing that Jesus endured the ultimate suffering when He died for *our* sake at the cross, that we may have life instead.

What a reason to rejoice! "Believing in Christ [also] means devotion to His purpose, which will always include suffering at the hands of those who would oppose Him. God enables such devotion" (*TLSB*, p. 2034). And as others, even would-be opponents, see our devotion to God's purpose, He is glorified.

"An imprisoned apostle writes to a persecuted church, and the keynote of his letter is: 'I rejoice. Do you rejoice?' Where under the sun is anything like this possible except where faith is, where the Holy Spirit breathes His . . . breath?" (*LBC*, vol. 2, p. 546). Only in unity, striving as *one* with the breath of the Spirit upon them, can believers stand strong in faith and courage as they face opposition and persecution.

4. How could joy in unity *enable* or *increase* joy in suffering? With fellow believers, how can you be joyful when faced with insults, suffering, or even persecution?

JOYFUL Challenge: *Joy in Unity:* Share a specific time you recognized the JOY you have in unity within the body of believers. Why is it so important to take notice of and rejoice in that unity? What's one special way you can celebrate unity, link arms and serve side by side with a few (or many) Christian family members this week?

Joy in Suffering: "Because of Christ, I can be joyful in the midst of _____." (Go ahead . . . what's on your heart?) How have you or others struggled or suffered lately? Take it to the Lord. Thank Him for His faithfulness in the midst of your suffering. Rest in His strength.

Week 2
Group Study

- ☐ **Review every JOY Theme from this week.** Take turns sharing a portion or favorite question, along with your answers, from each study session, and discuss.

  1. Joy in Seeing God's Hand

  2. Joy in Seeing Others Proclaim Jesus

  3. Joy in Answered Prayer and the Spirit's Help

  4. Joy No Matter What!

  5. Joy in Unity and in Suffering

- ☐ **Talk about your favorite JOYFUL Challenge.**

- ☐ **Share a JOY Snapshot.** See a general description in the Introduction.

Express JOY with a JOY SONG!

"I've got the joy, joy, joy, joy down in my heart." If you know this Sunday School classic, you're singing it now too, right? I always have a song in my head. (Go ahead, ask me any time, "Deb, what song is playing now?" And I can tell you.) And it's often a song of praise.

Praise can turn our mourning into dancing (**Psalm 30:11**); it helps us remember the reason we can always rejoice. A song can help us find joy in the ordinary things of life. God designed us to memorize more easily when words are set to song. (The Holy Spirit has given me recall of God's Word when I've most needed it because it's hidden somewhere in my heart and comes bursting forth in song. See **Colossians 3:16**.) As you face daily life with a song in your heart and on your mind, its melody plays even when you don't feel like dancing or singing aloud. Its tune keeps you tuned to the ever-present help before you, enabling you to cling to Him, the joy that IS Jesus (**John 17:13**). Revel in His presence, as reminded in songs of praise. Even when you cannot sense His presence, trust the truth of His promise, "I am with you always" (**Matthew 28:20**). So go ahead, "make a joyful noise to the LORD . . . break forth into joyous song and sing praises!" (**Psalm 98:4**).

Joy in Becoming like Christ

PHILIPPIANS 2:1-2

A STREAM OF LETTERS? OR ONE?

Have you engaged in writing and receiving a stream of letters with a friend, back-and-forth, back-and-forth, and each subsequent letter caused you to feel as if you were picking up right where the last one left off, practically mid-sentence? I still have a special stream of letters like this with one such friend, sent and received the summer after I graduated from high school. My friend's night job provided idle hours, and she used them to pen one long, ongoing letter to me, sent in segments. I would laugh as I opened a letter to the words, "Anyway..." or "As I was saying..."

READING THE LETTER

> So if there is any encouragement in Christ, any comfort from love, any participation in the Spirit, any affection and sympathy, complete my joy by being of the same mind, having the same love, being in full accord and of one mind. (**Philippians 2:1-2**)

We're reading Paul's joyful letter a little at a time, and too easily, we break it up as though it were several letters. When we pause between readings, and especially at major break points set for us—like chapters—we tend to start over, as if we're reading a whole new letter. I love how **Philippians 2** begins with "So..."

Special Delivery
When the Bible canon was established, both Testaments were in organized form, but it was one thousand years later that something close to our modern chapter and verse system was commonly used. Sometimes, a chapter or verse number can interrupt a train of thought, but the benefits of the system for finding, studying, and memorizing Scripture far outweigh any potential confusion or interruption (see Rau).

It's imperative we recognize that Paul continues with the same thought, a progression from the exhortations and encouragement he gives at the close of **chapter 1**. He knows the believers are facing strong opposition, and he's telling them how they can stand firm. What do they most need to hear now?

What could be better than an affirmation of who they are and what they've received?! I like to refer to Paul's first statement in **chapter 2** as a rhetorical one, since that's the best way we can put our English translation "if" to work in the first sentence: "So if there is any . . ." Paul begs the question, further emphasizing the facts, as if to say, "*since* you have received all this in Christ"!

ENCOURAGEMENT IN CHRIST!

1. As believers already, they are "in Christ"! What does this mean for the first readers of this letter? for us? How is the same phrase defined and explained in **Romans 8:1–2**?

   There's now no condemnation for those who are of Christ. Cause through Christ the Spirit set me free from the law of sin + death.

   We are united with Christ. We enjoy a personal relationship with the One who chose us and redeemed us from our sins. We are ONE with Him! He lives in us. "In Him we live and move and have our being" (**Acts 17:28**). *"We are his offspring"*

2. From this relationship come all of these benefits of salvation. Look again at **Philippians 2:1–2**. What do we receive from Christ? After filling in these benefits, circle one you're especially thankful for today; pause and pray with joy that it's yours in Christ.

   any encouragement _____ from being united with Him.

   comfort _____ from His redeeming love, demonstrated at the cross for our forgiveness of sins and for our salvation. (The same love spoken of in **1:9**.)

   Participation in (fellowship with) the ___*Spirit*___, who lives in us by faith.

   affection _____ and ___*Sympathy*___ = deep tenderness and compassion.

3. In **verse 2**, Paul implies what he has stated again and again to the Philippians: he is filled with JOY. What will *complete* the joy he already has? (This happens in response to God's amazing provision in Christ, flowing out of our unity with Him and all that we receive from Him.)

4. In **John 15:11**, Jesus said, "These things I have spoken to you, that My joy may be in you, and that your joy may be full." Looking at "these things" in the context of **John 15:1–10**, how does Christ's desire that His followers' joy be full compare with Paul's challenge to Christ's followers to complete his joy?

   By obeying his commands

UNITY IN THE BODY OF CHRIST!

Our unity with Christ makes possible our unity with one another. We desire to grow more like Jesus, seeking to imitate Him, handing out the same benefits we have received. We pour into others what He has so richly poured into us. Like the Philippians, we face opposition and suffer hurt, and we desperately need words of comfort and consolation from fellow believers, that we may remain firm, linked arm-in-arm in spiritual fellowship to stay the course as we face the hatred of opponents.

Being "of one mind" does not mean we are all going to think exactly alike (and that's a good thing), but that we have one and the same purpose: living and sharing the Gospel. We have the same desire to work together and serve one another, as *one* in Him. And most of all, we love as He loves us: "Therefore be imitators of God, as beloved children. And walk in love, as Christ loved us and gave Himself up for us" (**Ephesians 5:1–2**).

BECOMING LIKE CHRIST: DAILY PRACTICE

Though we may be tempted to wonder how God could be shaping us into Christlikeness on a daily basis, we can trust Him to provide opportunities for us and through us to others. Where can we offer *comfort*? *sympathy*? (When do we receive it, even unexpectedly, as it's shared with us in Christ's love?) How can we *participate in the Spirit*, in prayer for others and as we grow in God's Word? Whom will we encounter, that we may *encourage* them? And with whom can we share Christ's *affection* by our words and actions?

Will we miss opportunities to share Christ more boldly on an average day? Yes. Are each of us a work in progress? God says so. (Remember **Philippians 1:6**?) By His grace, He provides new opportunities tomorrow. May we embrace everyday opportunities as part of God's plan for us to practice Christlikeness, to *grow* in His likeness, to live our witness for Him.

JOYFUL Challenge: Start making a JOY list. Begin listing "benefits of salvation" like these from **Philippians 2:1**. These are just some of the many "fruits" you can hand out to others because they're yours in Christ, by His grace! (Add to your list the fruits from **Galatians 5:22–23,** if you'd like.) Then, attach names, interactions, or events from your day or week as they connect with opportunities to practice Christlikeness in this way. Finally, rejoice! Look at your list and thank Jesus for all the ways you're growing in His grace, becoming more like Him.

Joy in Humility
PHILIPPIANS 2:3-4

LOVE LETTER

My beloved pastor emeritus told a story involving a pretty fifth grade girl, a love letter, and a lesson in humility, all taking place in an early 1940s classroom in Brooklyn. He thought this pretty girl was the bee's knees, and that Valentine's Day, he was proudly certain she felt the same when he found an envelope on his desk with a homemade valentine inside. He was feeling smug until Miss Bee's Knees walked up with a look of panic on her face. She promptly snatched her words of affection from his hands and let him know they were meant for someone else. In a few minutes, this fifth grade boy's feelings plummeted from pride and conceit to humility.

How smug, how proud we are too. We give much thought to our own feelings (priorities, achievements, even to what "good" Christians we are) and little to no thought of others' feelings. You or I think *we're* the bee's knees . . . until we're convicted by the truth of our sin in our conceit. Thank the Lord, He doesn't snatch His Word of grace and affection from our hands. Every word in His love letter was meant for us to read and humbly receive as our own, by faith.

READING THE LETTER

> Do nothing from selfish ambition or conceit, but in humility count others more significant than yourselves. Let each of you look not only to his own interests, but also to the interests of others. (**Philippians 2:3–4**)

Just prior to these verses, Paul has reminded the believers who (and whose) they are and all they've received in Christ, along with a call to unity in the body of believers, just as each is united in Christ.

Here, he continues, leading the reader to a beautiful climax. How is unity possible? Dr. Jane Fryar put it succinctly: "Humility undergirds their unity in the faith" (*TLDB*, p. 1605). And humility is possible only when believers live out what they've been given in Christ: encouragement, love, comfort, participation in the Spirit, affection, and sympathy (**v. 1**).

1. In light of the unity to which Paul just called the believers, what is the problem with selfish ambition? Recall the motives of the Roman Christians who wished ill of Paul as they proclaimed the Gospel. How may that have eventually or already harmed the unity of the Church in Rome?

   Selfish Ambitions promotes disharmony

Special Delivery
Selfish ambition is synonymous with the rivalry Paul talked about in **1:15–17** when he referred to the Roman Christians who were emboldened to speak the Gospel, but only for selfish gain, out of envy and rivalry.

At the center of our sinful human nature is SELF. The fallen world, our sinful nature, and Satan all tell us to "look out for number one" (selfish ambition) and to think highly of ourselves (conceit). (See **Romans 12:3**.) Both fly in the face of unity. Self looks inward. Unity links arms and looks forward and upward!

SELF-FORGETFULNESS

Self-forgetfulness, then, would seem an appropriate base definition of humility, wouldn't it? A humble person is not preoccupied with thoughts of self. "Count others more __*better*__ than yourselves" (**Philippians 2:3**). This does not mean you put yourself down (self-deprecation) or consider others more worthy of God's grace or forgiveness. (The truth is, none of us is worthy of His forgiveness—that's why it's called grace! We receive it freely and undeservedly in faith.) In Christian love for others, you're called to honor and esteem them, show them preference, and desire to put their needs ahead of your own. As my pastor-husband said in a sermon, "Humility is not allowing people to walk all over you, but allowing Christ to live in and through you, serving Him as you serve others."

Special Delivery
Humility can be defined as "unselved," free from thinking about yourself. Humility means not being prideful but also not being self-deprecating.

2. What does humility look like, as defined in the following verses? Write a phrase for each and then combine them for a fuller picture of humility.

   Romans 12:10 *Honor one another above yourself"*

   Galatians 5:13 *Service one another in love*

   Ephesians 5:21 *Submit to one another, out of reverence to God.*

   1 Peter 5:5 *Clothe yourselves with humility toward one another.*

Paul commends the Church in Ephesus to the same: "I therefore, a prisoner for the Lord, urge you to walk in a manner worthy of the calling to which you have been called, with all humility and gentleness, with patience, bearing with one another in love, eager to maintain the unity of the Spirit in the bond of peace" (**Ephesians 4:1–3**).

3. Underline words or phrases above that are similar to the counsel Paul gives to the Philippians. Write the Philippians verse reference by each. What stands out to you most? Now consider what it might look like to count others more significant than ourselves, practically speaking, in our everyday lives. Fill in applicable, tangible specifics:

Let someone else go first. _____
_____ Be Humble & gentle _____

Let someone have the bigger, the better, the last. _____
_____ Be patient _____

Listen first, well, and more than you speak. _____
_____ Be patient _____

Give to someone before all your needs are met. _____
_____ Keep unity of Spirit _____

4. Honoring others above ourselves and self-forgetfulness are both key to humility, so does that mean denying our interests entirely? How does **Philippians 2:4** coincide with **verse 3**?

JOYFUL Challenge: J.O.Y. = JESUS. OTHERS. YOU. In that order. ☺ Our lives exude joy when lived like this. A life of humility is not one in which you have fallen off; you're just put in the proper place, after others. And that place needs time and opportunity to be refreshed and refueled. This is not to be confused with a cultural view of making life all about YOU; it's to provide the nourishment and replenishment needed to serve JESUS and OTHERS most effectively and healthfully. Take time out and time alone with the Lord. Jesus modeled this (**Matthew 14:23**; **Mark 1:35**). Be refreshed! Return with God's perspective and the reminder of the truth that it's not about you, but about being the best YOU possible, by God's grace, as you serve your Savior and everyone He sends your way, and as you take good care of yourself.

Joy in Having the Attitude of Christ

PHILIPPIANS 2:5-8

POETRY OF LOVE

For our fifteenth anniversary, my husband penned a poem in lieu of a card, hand-delivering this love letter to me. It chronicled memorable events, recalled our shared growth in faith, and reaffirmed his love for me. Cory could have more easily written a regular letter expressing his sentiments and memories, but there was something more profound about each word, chosen carefully and placed in poetic form, that made me want to frame it, read it again and again, and set the words to song.

Incomparably greater is the poetry before us today and tomorrow. The message of Christ in this passage is at the heart of God's love letter, His Word. As we'll see, it chronicled the most memorable of historical events, revealing the extent of Jesus' love. Each word is profound and poetic—we should thrill in reading it again and again! These very words have been set to song.

READING THE LETTER

> Have this mind among yourselves, which is yours in Christ Jesus, who, though He was in the form of God, did not count equality with God a thing to be grasped, but emptied Himself, by taking the form of a servant, being born in the likeness of men. And being found in human form, He humbled Himself by becoming obedient to the point of death, even death on a cross. (**Philippians 2:5–8**)

Special Delivery
Christ's humiliation in poetic form is viewed by scholars as an early hymn of Christ. It may have been familiar to the believers in the Early Church (*LBC*, vol. 2, p. 544).

Previous verses lead us to this divine poetic masterpiece. Paul now shows us perfect humility, embodied and exemplified in Christ, the ultimate example and all-powerful motivation to live in sacrificial service to one another.

1. In our previous reading, we learned some essentials of a humble Christian life and attempted to define humility. But the definition cannot be completed without a description of Christ's humiliation. Only in Christ is a life of humility possible.

   a. Read **verses 5–8** above; find and mark all the words or phrases that speak of Christ's humility. What did He do? How was He found?

   He humbled himself
   He died on the cross

   b. Read the following verses and write one or more of the marked phrases that correlates with each verse:

   Matthew 20:28 *Gave his life as ransom for other*

   Luke 2:10–11 *Savior has been born.*

   John 1:14 *The Glory of one or only.*

   Romans 8:3 *Sin offering*

   2 Corinthians 8:9 *Emptied himself*

   Hebrews 5:7–8 *Obidience*

HE EMPTIED HIMSELF

Christ is one with the Father and the Holy Spirit. Fully God, and at His incarnation, fully man. When He came to us in human form, He did not give up His deity (divine qualities), but He did lay aside the fullness of the glory He had in heaven (see **John 17:5**) in order to come to us in humility to complete His purpose. He emptied Himself in order to fill us that we might be rich (**2 Corinthians 8:9**) and be made the righteousness of God in Him (**2 Corinthians 5:21**). "It was because of the fact that Jesus is true God that His loving nature moved Him to empty Himself, even to the point of death on the cross" (Eschelbach, p. 605).

ATTITUDE ADJUSTMENT

Let's examine this powerful poetry in **verses 6–8** in light of the call in **verse 5** to "have this mind among yourselves." To have the humble mind (attitude) of Christ means we must undergo an attitude adjustment, right?! (Ouch!) In our sinful nature, our attitude is anything but humble. So we ask for God's grace that

He may turn us around, powerfully working through His Word to give us a Christlike attitude of self-sacrificing humility and love for others.

2. We know already that a life of humility includes honoring others above ourselves. Looking again at Christ's perfect example, what else is needed for an attitude adjustment? What does this mean for you?

Living with a willingness to ___Humble ourselves___. Jesus taught us all about service: "The Son of Man came not to be served but to serve, and to give His life as a ransom for many" (**Matthew 20:28**).

3. Read **John 13:3–5, 12–17.** What is so significant about Jesus' act of service to His disciples here? What did He teach, in His words and through His humble service? This service preceded another, involving His greatest act of service. What was it? *The washing of feet.*
You should do as I have done for you.

"If our Lord put aside the magnificent glory that is rightfully His to humble Himself, take on the form of a servant, and become obedient to a humiliating death—all to bring us salvation—how can we not give up our puny pretensions to glory in order to follow Him in humble service to others?" (Gernant Dumit, p. 54). Ask God to give you humility and a heart for even menial acts of service; to see the same value in every person, for whom Christ died; to give up any desire for recognition or glory as you serve.

4. Again, what else is needed for an attitude adjustment? How could you use help in this area?

Living a life of humble ___obedience___. (See **verse 8.**) Jesus was obedient to the point of death, perfectly fulfilling the Father's will, dying in our place.

Even Death on a Cross

Death by crucifixion was a curse. According to Old Testament Law, being hung from a tree meant being cut off from God (*TLSB*, p. 2034). Write the words to **Galatians 3:13** here:

Special Delivery
When Paul added "even death on a cross," imagine the Philippians gasping. As Roman citizens, they had likely seen the pain, agony, and degradation of crucifixion. "The Romans crucified criminals by the main entry roads into a city in order to humiliate them and to warn those who entered not to make the same mistake" (*TLSB*, p. 2034).

Jesus was our substitute! He took human form in order to redeem us from the curse of the Law and its penalty of death. This is historic fact, proclaimed to all the world; it is the heart of Gospel truth, which saves for eternity *all* who cling to it in confidence by God's grace through faith.

JOYFUL Challenge: The attitude of Christ is one of sacrificial humility and love. Recall the ways we talked about receiving an attitude adjustment, as we desire, by God's grace, to have the attitude of Christ. How can you place others above yourself, humbly serving with obedience today? this week? What if that service is menial? What if it necessitates interactions with people you might not otherwise associate with? What if you don't receive anything for serving and no one even notices? Maybe you're called to change diapers, help someone with physical or mental challenges, clean for another family, serve on a community action team, or give to someone even if it means you survive with less. Examine your heart, providing honest responses to these difficult questions and asking God for an attitude adjustment where it's needed. Let Him flood you with His joy as you remember His ultimate sacrifice for you and as you humbly serve others with the same joy.

Bonus: Do something anonymously and don't tell *anyone* you did it!

Joy in the Name of Jesus! He IS Our Joy!

PHILIPPIANS 2:9–11

THROUGH HIM, THE CHRIST

My children, like my husband, have penned some poetry of their own. Together, they drafted the following poem from the back seat of the family minivan one summer vacation. In words that surpassed their combined first- and fourth-grade wisdom (God was at work!), they wrote of all we receive because of Christ's humiliation and exaltation.

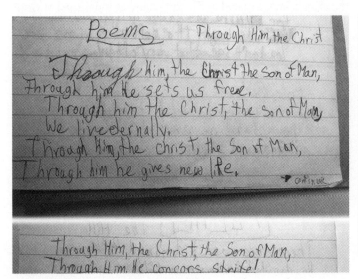

The original poetry hand-written by my children

Through Him, the Christ, the Son of Man, Through Him He sets us free.
Through Him, the Christ, the Son of Man, We live eternally.
Through Him, the Christ, the Son of Man, Through Him He gives new life.
Through Him, the Christ, the Son of Man, Through Him, He conquers strife!

I was impressed that they used the word *conquers*! And what a fitting word, since Christ conquered our greatest strife—our own humiliation and shame in our sin that had us dead in our trespasses (see **Ephesians 2:1**). But now, because He took all of it to the cross, we're very much alive in Him. Yes, by His death AND His glorious resurrection, He *sets us free* and *gives new life eternally*!

Reading the Letter

> Therefore God has highly exalted Him and bestowed on Him the name that is above every name, so that at the name of Jesus every knee should bow, in heaven and on earth and under the earth, and every tongue confess that Jesus Christ is Lord, to the glory of God the Father. (**Philippians 2:9–11**)

Verses 9–11 are a continuation (note another "therefore") of what was perhaps an early hymn in the church; the poetic words of Jesus' humiliation are followed immediately by His exaltation. All of it resounds with celebratory and mysterious truth. There is JOY in the name of Jesus.

1. Find and mark all the words or phrases that speak of Christ's exaltation in the verses above.

Hebrews 12:2 was written with a similar celebratory tone: "Looking to Jesus, the founder and perfecter of our faith, who for the *joy* that was set before Him endured the cross, despising the shame, and is seated at the right hand of the throne of God" (emphasis mine). Jesus could endure the agony of the cross, knowing the joy that would come through it: victory over sin and death.

2. Study **Ephesians 1:19–21**. By God's mighty power, He raised Jesus from the dead. How are the words of **verse 21** similar to (or even an expansion of) the exaltation of **Philippians 2:9**? How is His exaltation expressed in **Hebrews 1:3**?

   Cheerfulness, Radiance

3. Complete the following study helps:

   a. Circle (below) every action, every response to Jesus' saving love, everything we receive or do in His name, the name that is above every name. Read **Colossians 3:17**. What else do we do in Jesus' name? What does this say about our priorities and purpose?

   That we should do everything in Jesus' name, always giving thanks.

"Jesus is the Christ, the Son of God . . . by believing you may have life in *His name*" (**John 20:31**). "Repent and be baptized . . . in *the name of Jesus Christ* for the forgiveness of your sins" (**Acts 2:38**). The apostles "preached boldly in *the name of Jesus*" (**Acts 9:27**); Paul was "ready not only to be imprisoned but even to die . . . for *the name of the Lord Jesus*" (**Acts 21:13**). As believers, we "call upon *the name of our Lord Jesus*" (**1 Corinthians 1:2**) and assemble "in *the name of the Lord Jesus*" (**1 Corinthians 5:4**). We are washed, sanctified, and justified "in *the name of the Lord Jesus*" (**1 Corinthians 6:11**, emphases added).

b. What will happen at "the name of Jesus?" "Every ___knew should bow___ . . . and every ___tongue confess___ that Jesus Christ is Lord" (**Philippians 2:10–11**). When will this happen?

judgment Day.

ALL SHALL BOW

Have you wondered who Paul is talking about when he says "in heaven and on earth and under the earth" (**v. 10**)? Paul speaks of all created beings from all time. Wow! First, the angels and all the saints whose souls are with Jesus *in heaven*; next, all people living *on earth*; finally, the demons and those damned in hell. One commentator stated, "All shall bow in submission and make this acknowledgment or confession with either joy . . . or dismay. When that name and revelation shines forth in all its infinite glory, not even a demon in hell will be able to deny the Lordship of the God-man Jesus Christ" (Lenski, pp. 791–93). Another author put it this way: "*All* creatures in the universe will one day confess that Jesus is Lord. Believers will do so with faith and joy. Unbelievers and the demons will do so to their shame (see **Isaiah 45:23–24**)" (Gernant Dumit, p. 54).

4. Turn to **John 16:20–24**. Jesus prepares His disciples for His imminent crucifixion—His act of ultimate humiliation. With what word picture does He help them understand the range of emotions and responses they're about to have? How does Jesus speak of *joy*? What does He mean to ask God the Father *in His name*, and how do we do this today?

a) *With child labor" forget & be joyous.*
b) *By praying in Jesus' name*

Bonus: When we confess Jesus as Lord, what happens? When else does this happen (**Philippians 1:9–11**)? *Christ's return*

We'd be filled with the fruit of righteousness

JOYFUL Challenge: Have you thought lately about everything you do? In all your words and through every action, Christ can be at the center. Since you get to do everything in the name of Jesus, doesn't that make everything you do significant? It matters! How comforting and exciting, all at once. Maybe you'll write a poem for a loved one. Maybe you'll make decisions with students or make dinner for your family. Maybe you'll have a tough conversation with an employee or an amusing conversation with a friend. Your life is never without joy because Jesus IS your joy! The one who is exalted has given you life in His name. Daily, you and I fall short in our attempt to do everything in Jesus' name, but daily He forgives. He picks us up again, empowering us to live for Him again. The joy of OUR salvation is Christ's joy—the reason He could endure the cross—because He knew the outcome for us. Whatever you're doing today, do it with JOY—in the name of Jesus.

Joy in Obedience / Joy in Exercising Our Faith

PHILIPPIANS 2:12–13

GENTLE INSTRUCTION

As a nervous mom prepared to leave her children home for the first time without a babysitter, she left them a two-page list of instructions. Most items began with "Make sure you . . ." and "Don't do . . ." ("Make sure you listen to your big sister"; "Don't do anything you wouldn't do if your father or I were home"). Following her instructions, she wrote them a brief letter. She praised them for the obedient children they were, reminding them that they'd gained their parents' trust and shown that they were ready for this responsibility. She was confident they would make the right choices, even in her absence. Then she encouraged them to do their very best together—to make God-pleasing choices, with His help.

You can almost hear Paul's loving fatherly tone as he continues his letter to his beloved children in the faith—his partners in the Gospel. It's as if he's saying, "Now make sure you . . ." and "Don't do . . ."; "God has you in His grip!"

READING THE LETTER

Therefore, my beloved, as you have always obeyed,
so now, not only as in my presence but much more

in my absence, work out your own salvation with
fear and trembling, for it is God who works in you,
both to will and to work for His good pleasure.
(**Philippians 2:12–13**)

"Therefore . . ." What is it *there* for?! This one word always
prompts us to peek back to previous words. In this case, the call
in verses ahead is for obedience to the same humility we learn
from Christ's perfect obedience. (It's like Paul is saying, "Since
Christ was obedient, you also must be obedient.") Clearly, the
Church in Philippi has faithfully obeyed God's commands, as
shared and taught by Paul. (See **Romans 1:5; 15:18**.) He saw, firsthand, their obedience when he was with them during his second
and third missionary journeys. The hand of God was upon them.

1.   Consider these questions about obedience:

a.   Are you obedient to God—taking Him at His Word—
even when that means forgiving (**Colossians 3:13**), turning
the other cheek (**Matthew 5:39**), or praying for your enemies (**Matthew 5:44**)? What if it means listening to authority even when you don't like what they have to say (**Romans
13:1–7**)? What if obeying means you take the unpopular position and you're teased, mocked, or insulted for it (**1 Peter
4:14**)? What gives you peace in your struggle with obedience?

To know that God is in control.

b.   Where is God calling you to greater obedience, and how
is it possible? Has something jumped out at you in the Word,
convicting you of your failure to obey in a specific area or directing you away from something you've been tempted by?
Maybe, instead, God is leading you toward something new
or different, desiring your trust and obedience to follow.
Pray. Write about it. Share, if you can.

Special Delivery
Obedience means
a complete, willing
response to God,
that you hear God's
Word and act
accordingly.

MY BELOVED . . .

Once again, Paul expresses his joy in his relationship with
his family in Christ in Philippi; every word he writes is laced with
the love and affection he has for them. We are reminded of his
demeanor toward them as he exhorts and encourages them even
more.

LET'S WORK OUT

Let's exercise our God-given faith; let's persevere to the
end! "Work out" might sound like works-righteousness, but that

couldn't be further from its meaning here. It is not an attempt to earn salvation but to grow and learn from God's Word; to be stretched and matured in the faith. "The Christian life is neither passive nor self-sufficient; it is neither fruitless nor saved by its fruit. Paul's admonition to 'work out' is a remedy for our fallen, lazy, and apathetic human nature" (Eschelbach, p. 606). May God the Spirit fuel us with the desire to work out, that we may produce all kinds of fruit!

2.   When you hear the phrase "work out" in modern speak, what does it often mean? What do you think of? How can we correlate this word picture (and others, such as *fitness*, *endurance*, and *strength*) with what "work out" means here in Philippians?

Move forward with our faith.

As Christ-followers, working out (serving and doing) are a natural outpouring of all that God pours into us by His grace. Working out results in maturation of faith and involves perseverance to the end (**Matthew 24:13**). "Salvation . . . expresses itself in an ongoing process [our daily sanctification] in which [we are] strenuously involved" (*CSSB*, p. 1819).

3.   Read **2 Peter 1:3–8**, as the apostle Peter also encourages believers in our growth and progress in faith. With what does he encourage us to "supplement" our faith in our daily walk? (See **vv. 5–7**.) How is this even possible? (See **vv. 3–4**.) What does this growth protect from? (See **v. 8**.)

Add to your faith goodness; to goodness knowledge; to knowledge self control; to self control, perseverance; to perseverance godliness; to godliness; brotherly kindness; & to brotherly kindness, love.

FEAR AND TREMBLING

The fear that Paul talks about is a humble reverence and awe toward our mighty Creator-Redeemer-Comforter! We tremble in awe as we humbly remember our lowly position before Him, as we intentionally focus (heart *and* body) on Him in our daily faith walk. We make more of Him and less of us as we continue to grow and mature in the faith, furthering our obedience, only and always by His grace for us in Christ.

GOD WHO WORKS IN YOU!

Just as the Holy Spirit produced faith in us through Word and Sacrament, so He continues His good work in us. How exciting, and how very relieving at the same time! I do not have the ability and I cannot in my own strength accomplish the work to which I'm called. Here, "work" is a different Greek verb than the "work" of **Philippians 2:12**. It translates to our English word *energy*. He gives us His *energy* as He works mightily and effectively *in* us and *through* us for His purpose. (In **Colossians 1:29**, Paul even expresses how he is "struggling with all His energy that He powerfully works within me.") And this reminder keeps my pride and thoughts of self-sufficiency in check. I'm humbled to know it's His work in me.

To Will and to Work

The will is the seat of *desire*; to work is to *do*. To desire *and* to do. Faith *and* action. The Lord gives us faith to desire and to do His will . . . to obediently serve for "His good pleasure" (**v. 13**). Divine action enables human action. "God's work in us leads us to press for a Christlike life" (*LBC*, vol. 2, p. 546). He is pleased when we have life to the fullest in Him (**John 10:10**); He is glorified!

4. What faith IN action are you called to? What "accidental" encounter with someone may be no accident at all? What ministry may happen intentionally and even when you least expect it?

JOYFUL Challenge: Some days, obedience to God's will is harder than others. Because I am blessed with vocations of wife and mother, I know that obedience, in part, means caring for my family. But a portion of that care is so daily, mundane, even dull. One day, I was up to my elbows in bubbly dish water and letting my mind wander. I glanced at the single three-letter word on the bottle of dish detergent and wondered what the soap company was thinking when it chose *this* name for a product connected to such a mundane chore. I asked myself, half in jest, "Some days, is JOY to be found *only* in a bottle of dish soap?" I mused that maybe if I slather myself in it, I will be *covered* with JOY . . . or if I fill my bathtub with its bubbles, I can *immerse* myself in JOY. I sighed as I recognized the need for an attitude adjustment and turned my face upward, confessing my sins and offering thanks (for food; for family!) to the Great Energizer, who enables my obedience and endurance in the daily and the dull. Where can you find joy in the midst of the mundane? How can you recognize it, and what will you say to God? (While you're at it, fill your tub with bubbles.)

Week 3
Group Study

☐ **Review every JOY Theme from this week.** Take turns sharing a portion or favorite question, along with your answers, from each study session, and discuss.

1. Joy in Becoming like Christ

2. Joy in Humility

3. Joy in Having the Attitude of Christ

4. Joy in the Name of Jesus! He IS Our Joy!

5. Joy in Obedience/Joy in Exercising Our Faith

☐ **Talk about your favorite JOYFUL Challenge.**

☐ **Share a JOY Snapshot.** See a general description in the Introduction.

Express JOY with JOY EXERCISE!

Could your JOY workout become a regular routine? Could your faith "exercise" use a boost? Do you need a personal trainer or coach, a workout plan or routine? While discipline is involved in making time and priority for daily spiritual exercise, the great news is in the amazing, guaranteed results. (And unlike physical exercise, this doesn't have to produce sweat; it's not merely something you check off your to-do list either.) And guess what? With every "move," you're becoming more like Christ (God be praised!). Seek an accountability partner and challenge each other to grow in the Word, using a daily devotion, a Bible reading plan, or a Bible study like this. Worship with fellow believers, "not neglecting to meet together" (**Hebrews 10:25**). Enjoy an active prayer life, lifting up praises, confession, and requests throughout the day—alone and with others. Listen to Christian music: "break forth into joyous song and sing praises!" (**Psalm 98:4**). Keep your eyes peeled for opportunities to talk about your faith and make the best use of every opportunity (**Colossians 4:5**), doing all in the name of Jesus. Trust me, there is unspeakable JOY in exercising your faith!

Joy in Shining Jesus' Light

PHILIPPIANS 2:14-15

KEEP SHINING!

I received a letter from my friend Melissa, who had joined me for a retreat where we studied Philippians. She was excited that recent events at her workplace drew her to the same verses we had studied together. Melissa sat in awe of God's timing, His Word, and His work, as she wrote to me about striving to rise above the grumbling and complaining around her. She received unexpected acknowledgment during her annual performance review with her manager, who had noticed something different in Melissa. Shortly after this review, she received an email from the upper-level manager, who called her a "shining star on the team." Grateful for the opportunity to be a witness at work, Melissa was affirmed ... and encouraged to keep shining.

Paul's letter encourages, affirms, and exhorts the believers to—you guessed it—keep shining! Melissa's letter shows that she is a modern-day example of someone who has taken to heart God's words through Paul.

READING THE LETTER

Do all things without grumbling or disputing, that you may be blameless and innocent, children of God without blemish in the midst of a crooked and twisted generation, among whom you shine as lights in the world. (**Philippians 2:14–15**)

Verses 14–16 provide an action plan for the humble obedience Paul has just explained in **verses 12–13**. Containing challenges and exhortations, along with grace-filled reminders of His work in believers, it's a call to work out—exercise—God-given faith.

1. As you examine each part of the action plan, write whose action it is. (Is it our physical action? Is it God's action or work in us? Both?)

   a. Do all things without grumbling or disputing *Don't complain*

   b. Be blameless and innocent *His action work in us*

   c. Children of God without blemish

   d. Shine as lights *By His grace*

2. What attitudes and actions did Paul speak against earlier (see **1:15–18** and **2:3**)? What does he warn against here? Do you struggle with either of these, especially among other believers or within the church? How could it negatively impact unity? *Envy, rivalry & self embition*

GRUMBLING OR CRUMBLING?

Don't you love autocorrect? As I attempted to text "grumbling" one day, it came out "crumbling." Only one letter was changed, but an entirely different word and meaning resulted. Or did it? In this case, maybe one is the unfortunate result of the other when we work beside fellow believers. When we grumble against God, we show our lack of faith and our discontentment with His will. When we grumble against one another, we may damage someone's faith, draw lines of division, or do a disservice to the entire ministry, displaying a negative example for someone who may not yet know Christ. Eventually, faith and unity may both begin crumbling. Paul wisely warns against grumbling and disputing; neither have a place among believers who are serving God and one another in obedience. In **2 Timothy**, he further exhorts, "Have nothing to do with foolish, ignorant controversies; you know that they breed quarrels" (**2:23**).

"BLAMELESS AND INNOCENT, CHILDREN OF GOD WITHOUT BLEMISH"

Where have we heard something like this before? Peek back to **Philippians 1:10**. On our own, are we capable of claiming pure innocence? Without one bit of blame? Free of any blemish? But what about when we try really, really hard? This seems an impossible command, and in our sin, it is. God in His holiness deserves and demands perfection from us, but He knows we fall short. That's the very reason He sent His Son, the only One who is perfectly pure, innocent of all sin, without any blame. We are completely covered and cleansed in Christ. Then, as the Spirit moves us, we hunger to do His will, fully devoted to Him and to His purpose for our lives.

When God looks at us through Christ, He sees His adopted child. (Isn't it beautiful that this blessed identification—*children of God*—is tucked between words that speak of purity and perfection, since it's by God's grace in Christ that we are cleansed, covered, *and* chosen?) We get to call the one true God our Father—Abba—Daddy (**Romans 8:15**). All because of His love for us in Christ. "See what kind of love the Father has given to us, that we should be called children of God; and so we are" (**1 John 3:1**; see also **John 1:12**).

3. Think about these questions in light of our verses:

a. What do you think "crooked and twisted generation" means here, in light of the definition given? Can the same be said of our generation today?

the People who have left
the Lord's path

b. Read **Deuteronomy 32:5**, Moses' prophetic words to the Israelites concerning their future disobedience—their fall *into* idolatry and *away* from the one true God. With what similar and additional words does Moses describe the people in this verse?

They have acted corruptly.

c. What does Peter say in **Acts 2:40**, and how does it reflect Paul's words here?

corrupted

WE SHINE HIS LIGHT

"As the Philippians willingly, without complaining or arguing, obeyed their Lord, their blameless and pure lives would contrast with the morally depraved world in which they lived" (Gernant Dumit, p. 55). As people of faith today, we, too, are called to live differently than the unbelieving world, and we can because God is at work in us.

We shine the light of Christ. When we receive His light, it fills us . . . and we sparkle. We shine! We can direct it toward others who need His light to flood their otherwise dark world. Some

Special Delivery
"Crooked and twisted generation." A generation is crooked when it "has left the straight paths of the Lord. Crooked in mind and in heart and thus in acts. . . . Truth alone is straight; lies are crooked and bend in all directions but the straight one. 'Twisted' emphasizes and intensifies 'crooked'" (Lenski, p. 803).

Special Delivery
The Greek word for *light* in **verse 15** is "used regarding stars, hence it means 'luminaries' . . . the context is that of contrast to the dark world, dark in its moral crookedness and perversity" (Lenski, p. 803). Luminaries don't shine for their own sake; they shine to provide light for others.

versions translate *light* as "stars"—so let's sparkle like stars, letting our Christ-light shine onto the people He has placed in our lives.

4. When even the smallest light glows in complete darkness, how does that light appear? Would those in the darkness notice it or be drawn to it? How is this a picture of what we're called to do? "In the same way, let your light shine before others, so that they may see your good works and give glory to your Father who is in heaven" (**Matthew 5:16**). Because it's His good works in us, we shine *His* light. Where are others' eyes drawn?

    to the our father in Heaven

JOYFUL Challenge: Draw or cut out paper stars, or find star-shaped sticky notes. (Find glow-in-the-dark products for added effect. ☺) Then contemplate: What is God asking or calling you to do to serve Him that you may shine His light into the darkness of your world? How can you be a shining star, bringing His joy into your work or classroom, while shopping or at home, in your travels or in your local community? Write one-word answers on your stars and display them where you'll spot them daily.

Bonus: We shine even brighter together. Who's next to you, and how are you being called as the Body of Christ to shine? Pray about this and plan a joy challenge as a team, a committee, or a church.

Joy in Holding Fast to God's Word

PHILIPPIANS 2:16

FAITH COACHES

My sons' high school track coach spent several months every year training and preparing his team. He pushed his athletes toward excellence, encouraging them every step of the way. Coach is a man of integrity and faith, and I'm grateful for his influence upon my boys, both on and off the track. He modeled his faith in Christ and wasn't afraid to share it. Every year, as graduation approached and track season came to a close, Coach presented senior boys with their awards and a special *letter*. Full of affirmation and challenges, the letter urged the boys to grow in God's Word—to hold fast to the truth in a world that would attempt to pull them down all kinds of crooked roads. To this day, Coach is proud and filled with joy every time he hears that a former student is walking in faith. God's work through him has not been in vain; my boys and many other young men are evidence of it, by the grace of God!

READING THE LETTER

> Holding fast to the word of life, so that in the day of Christ I may be proud that I did not run in vain or labor in vain. (**Philippians 2:16**)

"[Hold] fast to the word of life, so that in the day of Christ I may be proud that I did not run in vain or labor in vain." -Philippians 2:16

Coach encouraging my son Chris after a long race

Paul was the best kind of faith coach to everyone he met. He invested years of sharing the Gospel, teaching the faith, and preparing people for the most important run of their lives. He modeled his faith by his life, and he was all about sharing it. Already, we've seen a wealth of invaluable guidance from him in this letter, each word inspired and guided by the Holy Spirit, and always filled with joy, encouragement, and affirmation. Now, Paul urges the believers to hold fast to the Word of God—the Word that gives life.

HOLD FAST!

In the previous session, we looked at an action plan for humble obedience. **Verse 16** is such a pivotal portion that it gets its own session!

1. Take a peek back to the other portions of the call to work out—exercise—God-given faith. How do parts a–d of the action plan (in previous session, Question 1) hinge upon e (below), as revealed in **verse 16**?

   e. Holding fast to the Word of life (our physical action, prompted by the Holy Spirit)

2. When have you been tempted to take the crooked path of the world? How might you have fallen for truth that's been twisted or perverted to suit false ideas about God and His Word? Why does this question, involving yesterday's "crooked" and "twisted" words, have everything to do with today's verse?

By trusting in Gods will

Cling to God's Word, which gives life. Hang on to His promises, which find their Yes in Christ (**2 Corinthians 1:20**), and live according to them, by God's grace. Stand firm upon the Word, even as a crooked, twisted, and depraved world would question, mock, or hate you for it. Worldly people may ignore it; they may even pervert it or attempt to destroy it.

My dear pastor emeritus, Rev. Paul Rowoldt, shared with me a story from his seminary professor who grew up in Germany during the Nazi regime. As a teenager, he was present as the Nazis burned Bibles in the city square. He never forgot one moment: as the ashes rose with flames and smoke, he reached up and grasped a partial piece of a charred page. The verse, still readable, said, "The Word of the Lord endures forever." (See **Isaiah 40:8** and **1 Peter 1:25**.)

"Like Paul, our labor would be meaningless and of no use to others if we lived crookedly and perversely as the world around us lives. But God is at work in us, moving us to hold fast to His Word of life, by which He extends His image and kingdom to others" (*LBC*, vol. 2, p. 547). Only as we hold fast, growing in God's Word, can we reflect the image of Christ and shine like stars. Others see His light in us, and they are drawn to Him and His kingdom through us. The Holy Spirit works powerfully through the Word to show them their sin and reveal to them their Savior.

3. Why was it vital that the Philippian Church receive and continue to live out this action plan? Why is it just as vital that we receive and live by it today?

Because without God nothing is possible

When Christ returns, Paul hopes to be proud—not boastful, not thinking of himself or any kind of self-accomplishment—but proud of God's work accomplished through him in his labor to the beloved people of Philippi. It rings of a similar tone to Paul's words earlier in this letter.

4. Compare this verse (**Philippians 2:16**) with **1:6**. How does one verse help interpret the other? What portion of these two verses is almost word-for-word?

good work

JOYFUL Challenge: I want to be like Jeremiah, who said to the Lord, "Your words were found, and I ate them, and Your words became to me a *joy* and the delight of my heart" (**Jeremiah 15:16**, emphasis mine). I want to ingest God's Word, knowing He works miraculously through it, filling and instilling joy in me and in you too! How can you joyfully "hold fast"? Consider practical ways to be in the Word. Carve out a set devotional time in your schedule, giving yourself fun reminders to do it. (Consider seeking an accountability partner too.) Create a special space and have a Bible, devotional, or Bible study ready, along with extras like a journal, colored pencils, note cards, sticky notes, pens, highlighters, and chocolate ☺. Get creative with time and space until you find something that sticks. Keep your eyes open for devotional apps, downloadable studies, and more.

Joy in Living Sacrificially / Joy, Even If ...

PHILIPPIANS 2:17-18

TRUSTING GOD, EVEN IF ...

Sarah, a medical missionary to East Africa, recently wrote in her newsletter about a mission team that joined her on a trek to two refugee camps in Northern Kenya. Each morning, their team visited different homes and learned of the refugees' living conditions and challenges. "Listening to their stories wasn't easy," Sarah said. "These refugees have been through some pretty horrific life experiences. Many have lost their spouse, parents, or even children. Some were separated from family members, and several years later, they still don't know if their loved ones are even alive. Most had to flee their homes under the cover of darkness and travel countless miles without food, water, shelter, or even the concept of safety." Amazingly, they are people of joy because they trust God, *even if* ... "Refugees deeply understand what it means to trust God every single day for their daily bread. In difficult times, those who know Him turn to the comfort of Jesus Christ. Evangelism and sharing God's promises with friends and neighbors is a daily occurrence." These beautiful brothers and sisters in Christ are *living sacrificially*, their lives dedicated to Christ, by faith, much as the missionaries' lives are too. Sarah sought our prayers on behalf of the refugees, that they "would continue to find strength and joy through their faith in Jesus Christ, for their health and daily needs, and that they would continue proclaiming the Gospel."

READING THE LETTER

> Even if I am to be poured out as a drink offering upon the sacrificial offering of your faith, I am glad and rejoice with you all. Likewise you also should be glad and rejoice with me. (**Philippians 2:17–18**)

Paul is a person of joy, too, because he trusts God, *even if* . . . He had lived through some horrific experiences of his own. And Paul believes he will be martyred for the Gospel, if not imminently, then eventually. He compares the eventual spilling of his own blood to the Old Testament pouring of a drink offering. Paul's sacrifice, in life and in death, would accompany the Philippian believers' "sacrificial offering" of their faith. He commends them for their lives of service, the kind of lives to which he had earlier urged the Roman believers: "I appeal to you therefore, brothers, by the mercies of God, to present your bodies as a *living sacrifice*, holy and acceptable to God, which is your spiritual worship" (**Romans 12:1**, emphasis mine).

1. *Therefore.* Across the earlier chapters of Romans, Paul repeatedly shared the Law and the Gospel, proclaiming God's gift of grace and mercy in Christ. Now he appeals to the believers to respond. How? And what is a "*living* sacrifice" (since *sacrifice* usually implies death)? How can it be acceptable to God, and what does he mean by "spiritual worship"? (Remember, as you unpack these words, this is what Paul commended the Philippians for doing.)

We have new life by the power of Holy Spirit

Flowing out of the Philippians' faith is a sacrificial attitude and life of service. By the Spirit's work in their lives, these early Christians are full of fruit, sharing the love of Jesus and doing good for others.

Special Delivery
Old Testament drink offerings were a part of the sacrificial system commanded by God for sin atonement. They accompanied the daily animal sacrifice and were poured out beside the altar (see **Exodus 29:38–41**; **Numbers 15:5–10**; Lenski, p. 807). They foreshadowed the final, complete sacrifice to come— Jesus, the sacrificial Lamb of God, who laid down His life for the final atonement for *all* sins of *all* time.

2. Two words appear twice in today's brief passage, once in each verse. What are they? What's Paul's purpose for this intentional repetition? (In my little writer's world, I call it "strong repetition" when it's deliberate and serves a special purpose.) **Bonus:** Another word appears twice in **verse 17**; why? How is this another picture of being partners in the Gospel?

Glad & Rejoice

3. How can Paul be filled with JOY, glad and rejoicing, *even if* . . . ? What's significant about the comparison of his martyrdom or beatings to a drink offering that's poured out?

Sacrifice

GLAD AND REJOICE!

With a heart of joy, Paul is willing to live for or die by the faith for the sake of spreading the Gospel. If Paul is "poured out on the believers" behalf, he is glad to do it. I find comfort in the words of the prophet Habakkuk, and I read them with "even if" on my mind. While I might not be martyred or beaten for my faith, I may suffer, I may hunger, I may have to endure hardship. But "even if _____"—no matter what happens—may I be at peace. May my life be filled with the joy of the Lord, by the power of the Holy Spirit. I praise Him for my salvation; I am glad and rejoice in Him. "Though [even if] the fig tree should not blossom, nor fruit be on the vines, [even if] the produce of the olive fail and the fields yield no food, [even if] the flock be cut off from the fold and there be no herd in the stalls, yet I will rejoice in the LORD; I will take joy in the God of my salvation" (**Habakkuk 3:17–18**). Yes, I rejoice!

Pastor Jacob Corzine put it this way: "When proclaiming the Gospel by which you are saved leads to mocking or persecution—these hardly seem like times for joy. Except this: Christians . . . have a deeper, unending joy that belongs to every person who knows himself to be a child of God. This fact of who we are withstands all adversity, unchanged because it depends not on us but on the Holy Spirit, who lives in us" ("Joy in Adversity").

4. How is it possible that we might contemplate imminent death as Paul did? Read **2 Timothy 1:10; Hebrews 2:14;** and **Revelation 21:4**. Share in your own words what these verses teach you about death.

Eternal life

JOYFUL Challenge: What's your "even if"? Even if your prayers are not answered the way you hope; even if the cancer doesn't go away; even if you're rejected when you stand up for Christ. I urge you to pray, "Your will be done in my life, Lord. Even if _____, I will rejoice! Even if _____, I will trust You, God. Even if _____, 'I will take joy in the God of my salvation'" (**Habakkuk 3:18**). "Praying for [God's] will to be done can mean really praying for Him to give us the wherewithal to stand in the face of trial and say: 'I am a child of God, and though they take all I have, they cannot take my Lord from me'" (Corzine, "Thy Will Be Done").

Joy in

Serving Others

PHILIPPIANS 2:19-24

I COMMEND YOU!

I've been asked to write letters of commendation for teens and young adults. I get to praise their abilities and accomplishments, and more important, their faith and character, to prospective employers, scholarship committees, and mission advisory boards. Because I have been blessed to minister beside and mentor these young people—at home and in the mission field—I've developed special relationships with them. Several have sought me out when they've needed a good word. These standout young adults have proven worth to me, and commending them comes easily.

With joy, Paul commends Timothy to the believers in Philippi. Paul praises Timothy's wholehearted commitment to the Gospel work they share. Mutually blessed to minister beside one another in the mission field, they've developed a spiritual father-and-son relationship; they're close companions, as well as co-laborers for Christ. While Timothy hadn't sought out Paul for these good words, Paul gladly gives them:

READING THE LETTER

I hope in the Lord Jesus to send Timothy to you soon, so that I too may be cheered by news of you. For I have no one like him, who will be genuinely concerned for your welfare. For they all seek their own interests, not those of Jesus Christ. But you know Timothy's proven worth, how as a son with a

father he has served with me in the gospel. I hope
therefore to send him just as soon as I see how it
will go with me, and I trust in the Lord that shortly
I myself will come also. (**Philippians 2:19–24**)

1. What does Paul point out specifically as he commends Timothy to the Philippians? What enables him to know Timothy's heart so well? And what's different about the content of his commendation than many we may give today?

    Blameless and innocent

Mentors

Timothy is devoted to God's mission and to Paul, his mentor and spiritual father. Mentors have served Timothy well since childhood, as his grandmother Lois and mother, Eunice, taught him the Scriptures and raised him in a faith-filled home. It's likely that Paul picked up where other early mentors left off, and some probably overlapped. Mentors made a tremendous impact on young Timothy, and we would do well to follow in footsteps like theirs.

2. Sometimes your footsteps take the lead, and other times they follow.

    a. Who has taken a lead in your life, investing in you in a significant way and influencing you to be more like Christ? Could you refer to one or more of them as a *mentor*?

    b. Have your footsteps led another's? Have you been a mentor in the past, and are you mentoring someone now? If so, ask God for specific ways that you may best serve and encourage your mentee. Whom might you invest in today?

> **Special Delivery**
> Timothy was one of several workers who with Paul contended for the spread of the Gospel, but we know more about Timothy than the others. We know he was raised in God's Word by his faithful grandmother and mother (**2 Timothy 1:5; 3:15**), and he travels extensively for the Gospel as a young (**1 Timothy 4:12**) pastor, sent out on Paul's behalf. These references come from two letters written by Paul to Timothy, fittingly named for him.

Sending Timothy Soon

The Philippians know Timothy personally. In fact, he was one of Paul's companions when the missionary first set foot in Philippi (see **Acts 16:1–3**) and returned with him on a later visit. He has traveled extensively with Paul, sometimes staying behind to teach for a time, then catching up with Paul later, per God's plan. Recall that Timothy is by Paul's side now (**Philippians 1:1**). Here, Paul reminds the believers (**2:22**) that they know already how Timothy has proven his great worth in their joint service for the Gospel. They know he's a spiritual son to Paul. And now Paul hopes to send Timothy to them soon.

3. For what two reasons does Paul plan to send Timothy to Philippi soon? (How do you see, here again, Paul's affection for them?) Why can't Timothy go just yet? What does Paul mean, "I trust in the Lord that shortly I myself will come also" (**v. 24**)? (How is that possible, since he's in chains? See also 1:25–26.)

Because Timothy has served with him & faith

Special Delivery
Did Paul get to send Timothy to Philippi and receive a report from him? Yes! When the trial was complete and Paul was set free and able to leave Rome, he traveled to Ephesus, where he met Timothy and received the report (Lenski, p. 815). Can you imagine the joy in their reunion?

No One like Him

When Paul says he has no one like Timothy, he's referring to other Christians in Rome who have helped Paul too. While they're fellow believers, perhaps they lack the spiritual maturity to place the interest of Christ—the spread of the Gospel—above other interests (Gernant Dumit, p. 56). Their depth of commitment does not parallel that of Timothy, who lives out Paul's exhortations in **2:3–4**; not only does he put others' needs ahead of his own, but his interests are those of Christ!

Serving Others

God's work in our lives enables—even emboldens—us to serve our family, neighbors, co-workers, and strangers, as they have need. His grace and strength give us desire and sustenance for what we would not and could not do alone. "Christ's love flowing to us emboldens us to believe God will meet our needs. That faith frees us then to go about meeting the needs of one another. We focus, by grace, on serving others and find in that service *true joy* flooding our own lives" (*TLDB*, p. 1607, emphasis mine).

4. Think about how joy and service are connected.

   a. Serving with joy so often has a boomerang effect. We don't serve for the purpose of receiving joy. (After all, it's ours in Christ already.) But in focused service of others, we may find a flood of true joy rushing into our lives too. Write about a specific time when the boomerang effect happened to you and you were drenched in joy.

   Serving my grandchildren

   b. Read **Colossians 3:15–17**. Can you find three reasons why or how we can serve others? (Hint, look for one in each verse.) Explain your reasons.

   Because I do it in the name of the Lord.

JOYFUL Challenge: How often, when I serve, is there a part of me that seeks attention, appreciation, or an accolade for my "good work"? (Forgive me, Lord!) Then God works in my heart, changing my motivation to one of *response* for what He has so generously given me in Christ. (Thank You, God!) He fuels me with real reasons for JOY in Christ-centered, others-focused serving: (1) It allows me to use my God-given gifts to benefit someone else. (2) It will bring honor and attention solely to Him. (3) Those who benefit take notice of Christ in me, and they're drawn to Him. They may even be motivated by my humble example to go and do likewise. Prayerfully consider what a new (or current) act of service may look like in the days ahead, and anticipate true joy flooding others' lives and yours.

Joy in Honoring Others —

PHILIPPIANS 2:25-30

A Celebration in Honor

My grandmother could pen a letter like no one else. Her wise use of big words and her thirst for knowledge were the reasons our family proudly called her our "walking encyclopedia." Her letters were always full of grace and eloquence. My high school graduation gift from Granny was a *Concordia Self-Study Bible*. Enclosed was her gentle nudge: "When you have occasion for Bible study, perhaps you will find this helpful, as I have." At age 100, she penned my birthday card with these opening words, "Birthday felicitations, Deb! Perhaps I should learn to spell better before I use less-commonly used language, but I hope my version carries the idea. I have recently learned that standardized spelling is quite a recent development of our wonderfully diverse vocabulary." Ah, my Granny.

Granny's walk matched her talk: wise, knowledgeable, and full of grace. From a gifted young school teacher of the Dust Bowl to a hard-working farm wife and mother, to a centenarian with an unmatched quality of life, my grandmother served others continually and was held in honor by many. She stood at the bedside or the graveside of many loved ones, and she endured a great deal of suffering in her years, but she faced her days with courage, determination, and joy in the Lord.

My family honored Granny with a beautiful hundredth birthday celebration, and I hope to honor her life and the legacy she left for her family. I can only imagine the coming-home celebration that awaited her when she entered into Jesus' presence in heaven. She is with her Savior now.

READING THE LETTER

> I have thought it necessary to send to you Epaphroditus my brother and fellow worker and fellow soldier, and your messenger and minister to my need, for he has been longing for you all and has been distressed because you heard that he was ill. Indeed he was ill, near to death. But God had mercy on him, and not only on him but on me also, lest I should have sorrow upon sorrow. I am the more eager to send him, therefore, that you may rejoice at seeing him again, and that I may be less anxious. So receive him in the Lord with all joy, and honor such men, for he nearly died for the work of Christ, risking his life to complete what was lacking in your service to me. (**Philippians 2:25–30**)

We can imagine the coming-home celebration held in honor of Epaphroditus when he arrived in Philippi with this letter from Paul. This man of faith was always thinking of others. He had courageously come to Paul's aid and sought to humbly serve by his side, only to end up suffering with a severe illness. Clearly, he loved and longed for his family in Christ at home, as we see in his concern for them. I'm certain the believers in Philippi did just as Paul had hoped: they received Epaphroditus in the Lord with all joy.

Paul again writes words of commendation for a brother and partner in the Gospel, "giving the Philippians good reasons for welcoming such a faithful and helpful servant as Epaphroditus" (Eschelbach, p. 607). Before he even begins his list of good reasons, Paul honors Epaphroditus with a fivefold description of this faithful man and sacrificing servant.

1. List the five descriptors of Epaphroditus that Paul gives. What's significant about the order of the first three? And what's significant about the last two, in combination with the others?

Special Delivery
Paul talks about *sending* both Timothy and Epaphroditus, but the Greek phrases are slightly different. "This difference means that Epaphroditus is being sent home 'to you' whereas Timothy will soon be sent for a purpose 'for you'" (Lenski, p. 812). What a joyful gift for the Philippians to receive their brother, Epaphroditus. The only other mention of this humble servant is in **4:18**.

MORE THAN A MESSENGER

Epaphroditus was a dedicated messenger, sent from the Philippian Church with a special gift of support, but also and *especially* for the purpose of helping Paul and assisting with his needs while Paul is under house arrest. Here, *need* means need of a brother, fellow worker, and fellow soldier for the work of the Gospel. *He* was the Philippians' gift to Paul, far above and beyond the monetary support he brought with him (Lenski, p. 820).

Special Delivery

The Greek word for a messenger who merely brings a gift or report is different than the word used for Epaphroditus: *leitourgos* = commissioner; official public servant. This man was commissioned by a church to carry out service, and in this case, for Christ's apostle Paul (Lenski, p. 820).

2. It's no wonder Paul commends Epaphroditus as another example of a humble servant. Epaphroditus "nearly died for the work of Christ, risking his life" (v. 30) to help on behalf of the church, as its representative. How can we tell that he was others-focused? How do you think the believers back home had gotten word about his illness, that Epaphroditus would know they heard he was ill?

Paul expounds with an update, letting them know the illness had been critical, and now for Epaphroditus's sake and for theirs, he prepares to send him home—for their comfort and for his health. Again, we see Paul's self-forgetfulness as he places their interests ahead of his own.

3. God's mercy was demonstrated beautifully to both men. How?

4. Is Paul upset with the believers in Philippi when he tells them Epaphroditus risked his life to complete what was lacking in their service to him (2:30)? What does Paul mean? How can Paul say "complete" when Epaphroditus couldn't finish what he came to do?

He honors him

JOYFUL Challenge: Whom will you honor today, even in small ways? Is there someone you'd like to organize a celebration for? Maybe a deployed soldier is coming home; he has risked his life to protect your freedom, and you want to thank him in a special way. Maybe a missionary family you support is on furlough; you'd like to show your care and thanks to them as they share the Gospel in places you cannot. Maybe there's a hero of the faith in your midst who has humbly served behind-the-scenes for decades; you'd like to surprise her with special recognition that honors her and glorifies God. Rejoice over God's work completed through all these people on your behalf.

Week 4
Group Study

☐ **Review every JOY Theme from this week.** Take turns sharing a portion or favorite question, along with your answers, from each study session, and discuss.

1. Joy in Shining Jesus' Light

2. Joy in Holding Fast to God's Word

3. Joy in Living Sacrificially/Joy, Even If . . .

4. Joy in Serving Others

5. Joy in Honoring Others

☐ **Talk about your favorite JOYFUL Challenge.**

☐ **Share a JOY Snapshot.** See a general description in the Introduction.

Express JOY with JOY TALK.

Now that you can joy dance, joy sing, and get plenty of joy exercise, isn't it time for some joy talk? As in joy-centered conversation; what could be better! (You're already doing this in your group, whether you realize it or not. So let's get more intentional now.) On some level, joy permeates every conversation when the Lord is present, and He is! Holding fast to God's Word, we read Jesus' own words in **Matthew 18:20:** "For where two or three are gathered in My name, there am I among them."

Like the psalmist, may your mouths be filled with laughter and your tongues with shouts of joy! (See **Psalm 126:2.**) Follow the B.L.A.S.T. model below to discuss one of the days' themes, like Joy in Serving Others, and personalize this to the past week. And . . . go!

Have a B.L.A.S.T. in your conversations:

Be warm and friendly to those around you.

Listen carefully to what's being said.

Ask fun, open questions.

Smile when you talk.

Think of interesting topics to discuss. (Swindoll, p. 95)

WEEK 5

DAY 1

Joy in the Lord!

PHILIPPIANS 3:1

WRITING THESE THINGS AGAIN . . . AND AGAIN

My husband and I repeated certain words of counsel to our children so many times they could recite them back. One evening, our youngest was leaving the house and said, "I know, I know: Be smart. Be safe. Be a gentleman," and we hadn't said a word. (But we did smile back at him and give him a thumbs-up. He had been listening!)

Many times, I have gently warned or counseled my children, through letters and in conversation, to be on the lookout for lies. To be wary of those who would seek to pull them away from believing the truth. Some warnings and teachings are worthy of repetition. Why do we study God's Word again and again? We desperately need His promises, direction, and protection because we are regularly bombarded with lies, enticements, and dangers. There are some things we simply cannot say or write too many times, like these:

□ Remember who you are and whose you are.

□ Find truth in His Word. (And when you know the truth because you're reading and growing in it, you'll spot a lie a mile away.)

□ Because of your saving *faith in Christ, you have joy—rejoice in the Lord*!

(It's no problem for me to write these things again, and they're a safeguard for me *and* for you!)

READING THE LETTER

> Finally, my brothers, rejoice in the Lord. To write the same things to you is no trouble to me and is safe for you. (**Philippians 3:1**)

Special Delivery
The opening word, *finally,* in chapter three may lead us to believe Paul is nearing the end of his letter, making one last plea, but in the Greek it serves as more of a connecting word, like *therefore.* Sometimes, it occurs more than once in a piece of writing and doesn't necessarily mean it's coming to a close (Lenski, p. 826).

Rejoice in the Lord!

Following so much encouragement and several examples of humble servants to emulate, Paul circles back not only to share his heart but also to encourage his partners in the Gospel to *rejoice*. Lest they forget or fall into discouragement or despair during their trials, they need to remember they have reason to rejoice in the Lord. As we know already, joy undergirds Paul's entire message. Remember the joy in Christ that Paul has for them because they believe, because they partner with him in the Gospel? And just as Paul refers affectionately to Epaphroditus as his "brother" (2:25), he follows with the same term of endearment to all the believers. God's adopted children in Christ, they (and we) are all brothers and sisters—how sweet it is!

Wherever you are right now, pause, look up, and rejoice in the Lord! Praise Him for the breath you just took. Praise Him for who He is. Thank Him for this day, for the faith that's yours in Christ, for the opportunity to immerse yourself in His Gospel truth right now . . . and spill over with His joy.

1. As you rejoiced in the Lord just now, what was on your heart? What came spilling from your lips? What words overflowed in thanks and praise? Record it, just for yourself, here.

   Thank you! Lord.

The Same Message

What Paul says next is not a brand-new message to the first recipients of this letter. They've heard it from him before, and now he's reiterating a message they need to hear again, to keep it fresh on their hearts.

2. How can we tell, right away, that the message ahead must be of great importance? How will it help them, according to this verse?

Repetition in Scripture always serves a purpose; it's never redundant, but necessary for special emphasis. It draws us even closer, as if to say, "Stop! Listen! This is important!" (Paul's next words are crucial to the purity of the Gospel message. He will contrast lies with truth, safeguarding them spiritually, much as he did in 1:27-30, when he warned them against other opponents.) "Reminders of the truth provide safety against the constant assault of falsehood" (*TLSB*, p. 2036).

In **chapter 4**, we see more of Paul's repetition when he says, "Rejoice in the Lord always; again I will say, rejoice" (**v. 4**). Paul's joy overflows! He can't help but say it again and again, even in his suffering. And here at the beginning of **chapter 3**, even as he sets up a repeated message of warning for them, he does so with joy. It's his *joy* to offer protection for these persecuted Christians in the repetition of the most important things.

Our circumstances are certainly not Paul's, nor are they those of the Philippians. But we have our own times of suffering. Can we respond as Paul has?

3. Read **Romans 5:3–5**. When we "rejoice in our sufferings," what's produced as a chain of results? SUFFERING → _perseverance_ → _Character_ → _Hope_. Can you connect each of these qualities to a time of suffering in your own life or in that of a loved one? How have you seen God producing one or more of these qualities in a difficult time or circumstance?

JOY VS. HAPPINESS

Joy and happiness are often lumped together, as if one could define the other or as if they are interchangeable. We've seen across the first half of Philippians that joy is so much more! Happiness is a feeling that depends upon circumstances; joy is a fruit of the Spirit that's ours by faith despite our circumstances. Make no mistake, we are justified (saved) by faith alone. But *what do we do daily with the joy we've been given*? We make a choice every day (even minute by minute) whether to smile or frown, whether to bubble over with the joy inside or keep it contained. Whatever the circumstances you face today, I can tell you this: you are blessed with every spiritual blessing in Christ (**Ephesians 1:3**). And by the strength of the Spirit, you can be joyful and thankful in all situations (see **1 Thessalonians 5:16, 18**).

4. When might you have used *joy* and *happiness* interchangeably? How would you define the difference to a friend, as you understand it now? Where can you make a choice to rejoice today?

JOYFUL Challenge: *Spilling over. Poured into. Bubble over. Overflow!* Maybe it's just me, but these words from today's session would have me picture a bottle of soda. If you have one handy, go ahead and shake it up. Pop off the cap. Now watch the overflow! The joy of the Lord, filled to overflowing within us, stirs the desire to bubble over, spilling onto (maybe even drenching) others around us. Joy, like love, is a fruit produced in us by the Holy Spirit (see **Galatians 5:22**). Will we keep it bottled up or, by the Spirit's power, will we bubble over with an overflowing measure of fruit? Our attitudes and actions, our kind words, our genuine care and concern, and even our tears and laughter bubble over, causing others to say, "I want what she has." I pray that you have that kind of joy today, sister! I hope you hear these words from Paul, from God, and bubble over.

Joy in Confidence

PHILIPPIANS 3 : 2 – 6

CONFIDENCE ROOTED IN WHAT?

"Where do you put your confidence? Where do you think people go to seek confidence?" The questionnaire I sent to a large group of women produced a wealth of written replies. While the following list is not all-inclusive, it represents most answers women gave. (To clarify, a person believes they achieve confidence *because* of, *in,* or *as a result of* the things listed.)

- ☐ Successes and achievements
- ☐ Compliments and accolades
- ☐ Abilities
- ☐ Education
- ☐ Appearance
- ☐ Health/strength
- ☐ Possessions
- ☐ Job/status
- ☐ Relationships
- ☐ Knowledge

1. Today, we have questions to consider, even before we read Paul's letter:

    a.   While it might not be unhealthy to feel confident about one or more of these things (as they may be good gifts from God), what could happen if we allow our confidence to be *rooted* in them?

b. Based on the above sources of confidence, how could confidence be diminished or destroyed? (For instance, if we root our confidence in our success, what could happen if we fail?)

These are conditional sources of confidence, and if we stake our confidence claim in them, we could find ourselves disillusioned, discouraged, or devastated. Even the most powerful of these sources cannot alone provide the root or base for the unswerving, sure, and certain confidence we all crave and need.

READING THE LETTER

> Look out for the dogs, look out for the evildoers, look out for those who mutilate the flesh. For we are the circumcision, who worship by the Spirit of God and glory in Christ Jesus and put no confidence in the flesh—though I myself have reason for confidence in the flesh also. If anyone else thinks he has reason for confidence in the flesh, I have more: circumcised on the eighth day, of the people of Israel, of the tribe of Benjamin, a Hebrew of Hebrews; as to the law, a Pharisee; as to zeal, a persecutor of the church; as to righteousness under the law, blameless. (**Philippians 3:2–6**)

Watch for the word *confidence* in today's reading, this time in a different context than we surveyed and discussed (or is it?). Who are the "dogs"—the "evildoers" who "mutilate the flesh" (**3:2**)? Paul uses bold words to make a bold statement. These are Paul's opponents, legalistic Jewish converts to Christianity (Judaizers) who aggressively oppose the Gospel. They claimed that a man must be physically circumcised—follow the ceremonial Jewish law—before he could become a Christian. Under the Old Testament covenant, circumcision was a mark that set apart God's people. Under the new covenant established in Christ, physical circumcision had become no more than an unnecessary cutting (mutilation) of the skin (flesh). (Read Paul's words to the Judaizers in **Acts 15**.)

WE ARE THE CIRCUMCISION (PRAISE GOD!)

Paul contrasts the Judaizers of **Philippians 2:2** with true believers in **verse 3**. Note his use of "we" for all who trust in Christ as Lord and Savior. *We* are not marked by a cutting of the flesh any longer. (See **Romans 2:28–29** and **Galatians 5:1–6**.) But *we* are set apart as God's own people—marked *by Christ*—in our

Special Delivery
Confidence is feeling or knowing that you can rely on someone or something. It is a firm trust.

Special Delivery
"Dog" was the Jewish label for all Gentiles because they were considered unclean; Paul hurls it back at the Judaizers (Lenski, p. 828). Dogs were wild, filthy scavengers, roaming the streets and threatening people's safety; they were dirty predators, like evildoers (Eschelbach, p. 607).

Special Delivery
Paul's warning is worthy of repetition (**3:1**) for so many reasons! It's foundational to His message; it's central to our faith. Adding to the salvation we possess by God's grace through faith in Christ alone is a deadly danger to us. We are saved through faith *alone*, not faith + circumcision; not faith + obedience to the Law; not faith + works.

Baptism, chosen and redeemed by our Savior. *We* have a faith relationship with Him; by His grace through His gift of faith, *we* are believers.

2. Fill in the words following each "who" in **verse 3** to describe those who are the circumcision. After each phrase, explain further what you think that means:

   Who __worship__ by the Spirit of God = __and__ __glory__

   Who _____ in Christ Jesus = __in his work__ __Jw at__

   Who put __place in trust__ in the flesh = __Christ and his Love for us__

3. We all glory or boast in someone or something. Do we boast in Christ or in self? Let's take a closer look at Paul's status before he became a Christian. Read again **2:4–6**. Look for two sets of three reasons for Paul's former boastings of his confidence in the flesh for his salvation. The first three are his by heritage; the following three are his by achievement. Fill them in below. Let's call them **Paul's Impressive Résumé for Confidence in the Flesh.**

   ☑ ____Circumcised____ on the eighth day, a Jew from birth, following ceremonial law to the letter (**Genesis 17:12**).

   ☑ Born from one of the two remnant tribes of Israel: ____tribe____ of ____Benjamin____.

   ☑ ____Hebrews____ of ____Hebrews____, a pure-blooded "Who's Who" of the Jews!

   ☑ An expert in the Law, a ____Pharasee____, an educated and honored leader in the strictest sect of Judaism, known for the most complete observance of the Law (**Acts 26:5**).

   ☑ A zealous Jew, a ____persecuter____ of Christians (**Acts 9:1–2; Galatians 1:14**).

   ☑ According to the Law, ____righteous____ to the extent of outward perfection: blameless. (Understood as the means of gaining favor/right standing with God by the Law.) In his former life, Saul/Paul was faultless according to the legalistic standards of outward obedience. He saves this most-important resume item for last, though we could say Paul scored 100 percent in every area (Lenski, pp. 833–35).

No Confidence in the Flesh

By using himself as an example, Paul warns the believers about the Judaizers. (They have already invaded and wreaked havoc in the Galatian and Corinthian churches [Lenski, p. 828].) Paul cleverly notes his heritage, status, and achievements here, and (wait for it!) immediately denounces and contrasts all of them with the incomparable riches of Christ.

We could summarize the concept of "confidence in the flesh" and bring it home with this definition—possessing confidence only in weak human nature, confidence based upon these:

☐ **Pedigree**—Who we are in the world's eyes, by status, family, or name.

☐ **Personal Appearance**—What we look like to the world; how we "appear" to others.

☐ **Performance**—What we've achieved; success, by the world's standards.

Have we attempted to root our confidence in any of these? By God's grace, we let go of our fleshly confidence and rest in Christ, who alone—by His death and resurrection—provides the unswerving, sure, and certain confidence we all crave and need.

Not Enough

When might the world's call for "confidence" come crushing down on us? My friend Sarah talked to me about an honest conversation she had with a friend concerning a lack of confidence and the resultant fears, lies, and insecurities that leave them feeling "not enough." Not enough of a friend, spouse, mother, leader, or teacher. Sarah said, "We exposed those fears and lies, knowing they aren't true, and yet we face them with regularity."

Sarah and her friend are not alone in feeling "not enough." The more vulnerable Sarah is willing to be with others, the more she sees this lie on display in their lives too. "Taunting and squelching any ounce of joy, this 'not enough' syndrome is paralyzing, contagious, and wicked to get rid of," Sarah admitted. Then she tenderly spoke truth about fighting off "not enough-itis."

4. Look up each verse tied to the following truths Sarah shared, and receive them for yourself. Ask God to fight off your "not enough-itis" for you, through His Word, as it fills your soul:

> **Special Delivery**
> *Flesh* has different meanings in these verses: the physical flesh/skin that was removed in circumcision, and the weak, frail human nature that's unworthy of our confidence; it cannot save (*CSSB*, p. 1820). Similarly, *circumcision* is spoken of in the physical sense first, and then referred to as a circumcision of the heart in faith.

- Jesus has already WON. Rest in His victory. (**1 Corinthians 15:57**)

  Thanks be to God, He gives us the victory!

- Say this: "I am enough." Yeah, you are, because the "I AM" is enough! (**John 14:6**)

  "I am the way, the truth and the life"

- You lack nothing. Not one thing. He has provided everything you need and more. (**Psalm 23:1; Philippians 4:19**)

  The Lord is my shepherd.

- "Such is the *confidence* we have through Christ toward God. Not that we are sufficient in ourselves to claim anything as coming from us, but our sufficiency is from God." (**2 Corinthians 3:4–5**, emphasis mine)

  And my God will meet all your needs according to His glorious riches in JC

JOYFUL Challenge: For today's challenge, let's go back to the listed sources of "conditional confidence." We know already that our confidence for salvation cannot be rooted in them, and neither can our confidence in our daily walk (in our justification OR our sanctification). "If a person wants to be just before God and genuinely valuable, this can only come from the Work of God in us" (Eschelbach, p. 608). Some of these confidence sources may, however, *spring out* of our overarching confidence in Christ. For example, *achievement*. When we recognize something we've achieved as being a gift from Him, we can use that achievement to His glory. Make your own list; confess those areas where you've rooted your confidence in conditional sources; then rest in God's forgiveness. Choose one or two healthy sources that may, instead, spring out of your Christ-confidence and pray about how you have already (or could) use it to His glory.

You can use every God-given gift to honor Christ, serve others, and proclaim His love to the world. God can use your successes, awards, education, and so on for His good pleasure. (Remember, it's He who works in you—**2:13**.) But a confidence sought in them is really no confidence at all. His saving grace sets you free from being chained to that kind of confidence so you can live life to the fullest in Christ.

Joy in Being Found in Christ

PHILIPPIANS 3:7-9A

SPECIAL RECOGNITION

An official-looking letter arrives in the mail, and we gaze upon the opening words: "We are pleased to inform you…" or "In recognition of…" Our heart pounds as we continue reading about ourselves, our child, our spouse, or another loved one who's being recognized for something special. Maybe it acknowledges an outstanding achievement, exemplary service, or great grades.

Sometimes recognition letters arrive unexpectedly and we're honored and humbled when they do. Other times they arrive in response to an application or a résumé, and we're thrilled to accept this appreciation or reward for our efforts. And these are good things. But can you imagine applying for salvation, submitting a résumé and giving good reasons why you should not only be accepted but also be recognized and rewarded with eternal life?

If Paul had turned in his **Impressive Résumé for Confidence in the Flesh**, he would have received one beauty of a letter of recognition from a certain sect of scholars—the Judaizers! But what would it count for?

READING THE LETTER

> But whatever gain I had, I counted as loss for the sake of Christ. Indeed, I count everything as loss because of the surpassing worth of knowing Christ Jesus my Lord. For His sake I have suffered the loss of all things and count them as rubbish, in order that I may gain Christ and be found in Him. (**Philippians 3:7–9a**)

What would Paul's résumé count for? Nothing! Less than nothing. What he once considered an asset he now counts a liability. What he once thought was gain he now calls loss. Recall how Paul used himself as the example for anyone seeking salvation by their pedigree, personal appearance, or performance (3:4–6). He had once possessed the perfect "gain," if you will, for works-righteousness (an attempt to be justified or made right with God by works). Until, that is, Jesus called Paul (then named Saul) on the road to Damascus (see **Acts 9**), transforming a ruthless persecutor of Christians into a sacrificial missionary and follower of Christ.

SELF OR CHRIST?

Paul immediately denounces and contrasts all of his fleshly confidence with knowing Christ, His Lord and Savior. In today's reading, that's made clear.

1. Where salvation is concerned, Paul has been transformed from a place of so-called *self-confidence* to having complete *Christ-confidence*. Do you think there's an appropriate place for self-confidence in a Christian's life? Start pondering this question by listing other "self"-prefixed words. Then explain your thoughts. (Examples are included in the back-of-the-book answers.)

A COMPLETE CONTRAST

A faith relationship with Jesus is transforming! Paul uses repetition again as he stresses the night-and-day contrast between his former way of life, apart from Christ, and his new life in Christ, by faith.

2. In the chart, contrast Paul's former life and new life—his gains and losses—using his series of progressively more powerful statements (**vv. 7–9**). Based on the meanings of "loss" and "rubbish," what can we say about the measure of Paul's contrast and the urgency of his warning?

Confidence in Flesh	Confidence in Christ
Whatever _gain_ I had	I count as _loss_ .
I count _rubbish_ as loss	surpassing worth of _knowing_ Christ Jesus
I count all those things as _found_	I gain Christ and am _found_ in Him
Bonus: Righteous by the _law_	**Bonus:** Righteous by _faith_

> **Special Delivery**
> *Loss* (Greek *zemia*) means "damage" or "disadvantage." Confidence in flesh actually interferes with knowing God. Reliance on works for salvation is not only "useless and a hindrance, but [is] also harmful" (*TLSB*, p. 2036), damaging the soul. It kept Paul from seeing his need for a Savior. *Rubbish* = refuse; worthless and despicable (*CSSB*, p. 1820). This word was found in a papyrus with the Greek meaning "'rotten hay,' . . . no better than 'dung' (manure) . . . a stinking mess" (Lenski, p. 837).

Special Delivery

Surpassing worth! In his former life, Paul "surpassed" others his age in his "Pharisaic zeal and false Jewish merit" (Lenski, p. 836). (See **Galatians 1:14**.) Now, he has something drastically different and entirely true that surpasses all else: he knows Christ! This "knowing" is more than mere head knowledge; it's also heart knowledge— a personal faith relationship with the Savior.

ROOTED AND FOUND

Our confidence is rooted entirely in Christ and we are "found in Him" (**v. 9**). Knowing Jesus and being united in Him (**2:1**)—through Baptism and in our growing relationship with Him through the Word—surpasses everything else. Doesn't this truth cause you to jump for joy? Remember **1:6**? Paul tells us we can be *confident* that God—the Author of our faith—who "began a good work" (salvation) in us, will complete it—perfect it—in the day of Christ's return. (See also **Hebrews 12:2**.)

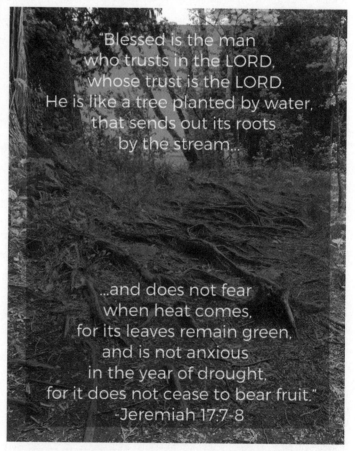

"Blessed is the man
who trusts in the LORD,
whose trust is the LORD.
He is like a tree planted by water,
that sends out its roots
by the stream...

...and does not fear
when heat comes,
for its leaves remain green,
and is not anxious
in the year of drought,
for it does not cease to bear fruit."
-Jeremiah 17:7-8

3. Read **Jeremiah 17:7–8**. As you do, note especially the *roots*. In whom is our *confidence* or *trust*? The words *confidence* and *trust* have the same Hebrew root word. To what in our lives could we compare heat or drought, and what's the outcome, thanks to the roots? How is this similar to Jesus' command in **John 15:1–5**?

DAILY CONFIDENCE

Because of the confidence we possess in Christ for our salvation and for everything we need in our walk of faith, our concept of daily confidence and its sources are like night and day too. (They're a complete contrast from the world's.) We touched on this in our last session, and now we'll view it from a different angle.

4. Remember *Pedigree, Personal Appearance,* and *Performance*? Flip those to: *Beauty, Identity,* and *Value.* All are found in your relationship with Christ. Look up the verses listed below and personalize what God says about you as you consider what you think of yourself. Is it in line with God's perfect knowledge *of you* and love *for you* in Christ?

Beauty = How you are viewed or seen, both inwardly and outwardly. **1 Peter 3:4**

Identity = How you are known; who you are. **Isaiah 43:1; 1 John 3:1; Galatians 3:~~36-37~~**
  26-27

Value = How your worth is measured. **1 Corinthians 7:23; Ephesians 1:4**

Get this: Your confidence does not change based on anyone's changing words or opinions of you (even your own) but on God's unchanging truth. There's no way it can be diminished or destroyed. Celebrate, sister, celebrate—jump for joy!

JOYFUL Challenge: Like most children, I always wanted my parents to be proud of me, and when they opened a recognition letter or a report card, I watched eagerly for their response. I wanted to be on the "A" list—in letter grades *and* in life. What's the "A" list in life? Achievements, Accomplishments, Accolades, Acceptance or Approval of others, Abilities, Appearance … you get the idea. But now I would trash everything on the "A" list if those things got in the way of my walk with the Lord. They gain nothing for the salvation that's mine in Christ. I've learned not to root my confidence in them for beauty, identity, or value. My life is "hidden with Christ in God" (**Colossians 3:3**) … and so is yours. Sister in Christ, you are *Found. In. Him.* Let that truth soak in a little more. Today I challenge you to quietly contemplate this in light of every "A" list item you've ever allowed to define you or measure your worth or beauty. Rejoice that Jesus lives in you. He chose you, knows you, forgives you, and loves you. And He has purpose for you too. The Almighty, All-knowing, Always-present Savior has you on the only "A" list that really matters!

Joy in Receiving Righteousness by Faith

PHILIPPIANS 3:9B

A LIVING LETTER

How is your life a living letter? I've given thought to this intriguing question as I write about Paul's Letter of Joy. What are people "reading" about you through your conversations, in your choices, by your attitudes and interactions? What do you hope they read? What do you want the takeaway to be? Where does your focus lie? Does your life letter include only facts ("This is what I did today."), or does it include your heart too? (Paul's contained both.) Your life is a letter that continues to be written.

If my life is a "living letter," I don't want it to be all about me. Sure, I would include my words and actions (the facts); I pray they would reveal "the fruit of righteousness that comes through Jesus Christ" (**Philippians 1:11**). I hope people would read all about Jesus, who gives LIFE to my letter, who forgives every poor choice and bad attitude; He fulfilled the Law perfectly in my place because I couldn't. And I pray that *my focus* would also be *their takeaway*: we are righteous before God by faith in Christ, our Savior. He is our righteousness! God's love letter to us reminds us of that.

> Not having a righteousness of my own that comes from the law, but that which comes through faith in Christ, the righteousness from God that depends on faith. (**Philippians 3:9b**)

We have Christ's righteousness *because* we are united with Him by faith (**2:1**), *because* we are found in Him (**3:9a**). Jesus lived "rightly" or perfectly. When He came to us in the flesh, He lived without sin; He accomplished what we could not. Dr. Michael Eschelbach put it this way: "The righteousness that comes by faith still depends on keeping the Law perfectly, but that perfection [in Christ!] is accounted to the one who believes. . . . Jesus exchanged His righteousness according to the Law for our guilt under the Law" (p. 609). "For our sake [God] made [Jesus] to be sin who knew no sin, so that in Him we might become the righteousness of God" (**2 Corinthians 5:21**).

1. Look up the following verses and summarize them in your own words, letting Scripture interpret Scripture as we continue to study this beautiful focus of our living letter: righteousness by faith.

Jeremiah 23:6 *Judah will be saved & Israel will be in safety. The Lord is our righteousness*

Romans 3:21–26 *The righteousness from God comes trugh faith in Jesus*

Galatians 2:21 *The grace of God which is righteousness makes Christ death justifiable?*

A STARK CONTRAST

2. Circle "comes" and "righteousness" in today's verse; each occurs twice. Note the stark contrast between the two kinds of righteousness. Which is impossible to attain and why? Which is possible and how?

NOT a righteousness of __my__ __own__ = my doing; comes __from__ __the law__

BUT a righteousness __from__ __God__ = His doing; comes __by faith__

One more key word appears twice. Do you see it? FAITH—worthy of repetition. We have righteousness by means of our faith in Jesus Christ. We have salvation because of this faith. We live our lives today and for eternity by faith. God's gift of faith, founded and perfected by Jesus Himself, is absolutely essential for righteousness. (See **Hebrews 12:2**.)

Special Delivery

Righteousness (Greek *dikaiosyne*) means being right, in accordance with the Law. It has the same Greek root as *justify*. God is holy and right in His nature because He is God. He makes His righteousness known to people through His work on their behalf. Jesus is our righteousness, the One who puts us in a right relationship with God through faith (*CCBH*, p. 611).

Special Delivery

Justify—"To declare righteous and free from sins and to absolve a person from eternal punishment for the sake of Christ's righteousness, which is credited by God to faith" (*TLSB*, p. 2037). (See **Galatians 2:16**.)

For I am not ashamed of the gospel, for it is the power of God for salvation to everyone who believes, to the Jew first and also to the Greek. For in it the righteousness of God is revealed from faith for faith, as it is written, "The righteous shall live by faith." (**Romans 1:16–17**)

3. In the past several Philippians verses and here in Romans, we read numerous strong words. We can almost hear Paul shout them. Why would Paul be so adamant and boldly repetitive to clarify righteousness by faith alone? to maintain the purity of the Gospel?

4. There is a careful distinction between the Law and the Gospel here; righteousness is ours by faith alone. So where do works come in? Sometimes we're afraid to talk about our works for fear there's confusion that we're attempting to gain favor with God through them, but rightly understood, works are an integral part of our daily walk. Read **Ephesians 2:8–10** and **James 2:14–18**. Write what you learn.

Our faith has to be accompanied by deeds.

God the Spirit works in and through us, producing the fruit we talked about earlier, so works (fruit) are a natural outpouring of the faith within us.

No Condemnation!

The first verse of the following passage was set to song by gifted musicians in one of our former churches. I know the words by heart, thanks to their tune. I hope you'll hum your own made-up tune to a few of these grace-filled words. Circle—and sing—those that stand out most:

There is therefore now no condemnation for those who are in Christ Jesus. For the law of the Spirit of life has set you free in Christ Jesus from the law of sin and death. For God has done what the law, weakened by the flesh, could not do. By sending His own Son in the likeness of sinful flesh and for sin, He condemned sin in the flesh, in order that *the righteous requirement of the law might be fulfilled in us,* who walk not according to the flesh but according to the Spirit. (**Romans 8:1–4**, emphasis mine)

JOYFUL Challenge: Your life IS a living letter, so why not practice writing a page (literally) today? Hit the highlights, share your actions and your heart as if you're writing to a close friend and you'd like her to know everything that's important about this day. Remember your focus: your living-letter life is completely covered in Christ—in His righteousness, draped over you as the robe described in **Isaiah 61:10**. He redeems your sins; He guides your words and actions; He gives LIFE to your letter. Oh, what incredible JOY there is in receiving His righteousness by faith!

Joy in Sharing Jesus' Suffering ... and Resurrection Power

PHILIPPIANS 3:10-11

A CLOSE WALK WITH THE SAVIOR

Recently, I pulled out my first prayer journal, a gift from my best friend nearly twenty years ago. God used her to energize me in my faith walk—to hunger for more time in His Word and in prayer, to desire a close walk with my Savior. Writing in my prayer journal was like writing letters to God. ☺ I smiled through tears at this entry: "Increase my trust in You. Thank You for Your forgiveness and mercy. What an awesome God I serve! Work Your Holy Spirit in me to desire Your best and seek that every day." Thanks be to God, my desires haven't changed and I've grown more confident in these past twenty years, knowing that the same power that raised Jesus from the grave lives and works in me (**Ephesians 1:19–20**), drawing me closer to Him and transforming me continually into His image.

READING THE LETTER

That I may know Him and the power of His resurrection, and may share His sufferings, becoming like Him in His death, that by any means possible I may attain the resurrection from the dead. (**Philippians 3:10-11**)

Paul knows Jesus' resurrection power, and his desires reflect that clearly. To more fully grasp the compelling words of today's verses, though, we need to remember all that Paul counts as loss and the incomparable gain he has in Christ. The purpose for Paul's *instant* loss of everything he once held dear is that *in the same instant* (at his conversion, **Acts 9**), he gained a Savior! In that instant, as Christ called Paul out of the darkness and into His marvelous light, he was *found*. At that very moment, Paul received the righteousness of Christ by faith.

Paul's heart is full! He desires an intimately close walk with His Savior. And he wants this incomparably more than anything else. In **Philippians 3:10**, Paul is restating God's purpose for him, which was accomplished at his conversion (Lenski, p. 841). That's how Paul first came to "know Him and the power of His resurrection." Jesus said, "For I will show him how much he must suffer for the sake of My name" (**Acts 9:16**). That's how Paul would share Christ's sufferings.

THE POWER OF HIS RESURRECTION

"The power of His resurrection is the seal of His redemption." Think about the weight of those words. Jesus' resurrection power secured the victory He won for Paul—and for us—at the cross. He conquered sin, death, and the devil. And *His* resurrection makes *our* resurrection possible—a reality for all who believe!

There is no greater joy than this. Christ Himself, just before His crucifixion, comforted His disciples as He prepared them for what was to come: "So also you have sorrow now, but I will see you again, and your hearts will rejoice, and no one will take your joy from you" (**John 16:22**). They saw Him again in His full glory, resurrected. No one could take away their joy, and no one can take away ours. This is the joy of our salvation; joy in the new life we have in Him.

1. In **Ephesians 1**, Paul explains Jesus' resurrection power, describing "the immeasurable greatness of His power toward us who believe, according to the working of His great might that He worked in Christ when He raised Him from the dead" (**Ephesians 1:19-20**). "Paul wants to experience the power of God that raised Jesus from the dead, the power that works in believers to bring them closer to Christ and transform them into His image" (Gernant Dumit, p. 58). Write about a time when you saw this power at work.

Special Delivery
On the road to Damascus, Jesus came in a blinding light to the persecutor Saul, also known as Paul. Saul saw the risen Lord in the power of His resurrection. "This power of Christ's resurrection became Paul's personal, blessed *gnosis* (Greek: knowledge). He was made to know Christ Jesus as 'my Lord.' ... The power of His resurrection is the seal of His redemption" (Lenski, pp. 841–42).

SHARE HIS SUFFERINGS

Luke says, "Was it not necessary that the Christ should suffer these things and enter into His glory?" (**Luke 24:26**). Paul says to the Church in Corinth: "For as we share abundantly in Christ's sufferings, so through Christ we share abundantly in comfort too" (**2 Corinthians 1:5**). Sharing Jesus' sufferings means a willingness to suffer as a result of faith in Him, even if that suffering is persecution or death.

2. Look at **2 Corinthians 11:23–28** and **12:10** and list some of Paul's sufferings. When did the Philippians see him in some of this suffering?

Beaten, stoned, jailed, lost at sea, starve, confronted by thieves. In jail

3. Compare Paul's words in **Romans 8:16–18** to Peter's words in **1 Peter 4:13**; both shared Jesus' sufferings as His apostles. What happens as a *result* of suffering with Jesus, and how does it compare with suffering itself? What does sharing Christ's sufferings look like today? How can we respond?

So that we may be overjoyed when his glory is revealed. Persecuted by constant reminders, + questions of Phil. 4

"Rejoice," Peter says, much like Paul does, especially in Philippians. It's an honor to share Christ's sufferings, no matter how horrible the suffering is, because we know that He suffered incomparably more and He endured it *for us*—to save us. We can rejoice again that through our suffering, by our life and witness, Jesus' glory is revealed!

BECOMING LIKE HIM IN HIS DEATH

We are continually being transformed into His image, even "becoming like Him in His death" (**Philippians 3:10**). "A Christian, as the name is meant to indicate, will follow the pattern of Jesus, laying down his or her life for others" (*TLSB*, p. 2037).

In **Galatians 2:20**, you can almost hear Paul exclaiming, "I have been crucified with Christ. It is no longer I who live, but Christ who lives in me. And the life I now live in the flesh I live by faith in the Son of God, who loved me and gave Himself for me." Through our Baptism, we have died with Christ and have been raised to new life in Him! (See **Romans 6:3–4**.) Peter said it like this, "He Himself bore our sins in His body on the tree, that we might die to sin and live to righteousness. By His wounds you have been healed" (**1 Peter 2:24**). Daily we die to our sin as we remember our Baptism. In this, too, we can rejoice.

RESURRECTION FROM THE DEAD

While Paul knows he must keep striving with his eyes on Christ, he is certain of his salvation (see **Philippians 1:23**). "By any means possible" doesn't imply that he doubts it. It indicates that he is unsure by which means it will be complete. He expresses expectation but admits uncertainty in the "how." Will he die as a martyr with his blood poured out (**2:17**) or as a free man? Paul knows "his body will sleep in peace until Christ awakes it . . . at the last day" (Lenski, pp. 844–45). At the day of Christ's return, at the *final* resurrection, our bodies will be raised in glory. This is without a doubt the greatest anticipation for all believers.

4. Read **1 Thessalonians 4:13–17**, a beautiful description of the final resurrection. List the details that stand out to you; some may even answer questions you've had concerning this Great Day of the Lord. (For further study, read **1 Corinthians 15**.) *God will bring with Jesus all of those who have died. When He comes down from Heaven with a loud command all who died to rise, all of those who are still alive will get on the clouds with them to meet the Lord in the air*

God, who has given us eternal souls, will raise our bodies from the dead to a fullness of life beyond our imagination. Our bodies will be like His glorified body: in a perfect state, without possibility of disease or decay. On that day, God will make all things new—all things right. Rejoice!

JOYFUL Challenge: Our Savior and His purpose for us are at the center of our being and why we do all we do. As our Gospel-sharing lives advance the kingdom, we may be persecuted because of Jesus. The world hates Christ, so it will hate us because we are connected to Him. (See **John 15:18–21**.) Prayerfully consider how you will respond if you are persecuted, ridiculed, mocked, hated, or insulted because of your faith. Can you, safe in God's grip, count it an honor if you should suffer for His sake? May you, by the Holy Spirit's power, remain loyal to your Lord no matter the cost. With Jesus' joy, pray that your suffering may lead a lost person to Christ or embolden a believer to share her faith without fear. Rejoice in your salvation, sister! Rejoice in the final resurrection that awaits.

Week 5
Group Study

☐ **Review every JOY Theme from this week.** Take turns sharing a portion or favorite question, along with your answers, from each study session, and discuss.

1. Joy in the Lord!

2. Joy in Confidence

3. Joy in Being Found in Christ

4. Joy in Receiving Righteousness by Faith

5. Joy in Sharing Jesus' Suffering . . . and Resurrection Power

☐ **Talk about your favorite JOYFUL Challenge.**

☐ **Share a JOY Snapshot.** See a general description in the Introduction.

Express JOY with a JOY CREATION.

How can you express your joy creatively? (Yes, you have at least a few creative bones in your body because God designed you with unique abilities and means of creative expression.) In praise to your Master Craftsman for the creation that is YOU, express your joy today! Not feeling particularly joyful? Author Luci Swindoll said some of the most amazing art and brilliant compositions were born of the artists' or composers' deepest grief, "but look at the joy they brought to the rest of the world" (Swindoll, p. 74). How might creating something lift your spirits and enable you to exude joy, blessing others as you do? Share in your group at least one way you express yourself creatively, and either combine your gifts to make a group creation or individually commit to expressing your *joy in the Lord* in one or more of these areas this week. Bring it with you, perform it, or share a photo of it, if possible, at your next group Bible study.

Bonus: Incorporate the word *joy* somehow into your creation!

Art: drawing, painting, sculpting, sketching, coloring

Craft: using any number of media to create something new or re-purposed by sewing, gluing, stapling, cutting, painting, welding

Music: singing, playing, writing lyrics, composing music, performing, listening (and singing along!)

Food: baking, cooking, preserving, grilling, creating new recipes, adapting old ones

More: photography, interior decor, gardening, landscaping, building, entertaining/hospitality

Joy in Pressing Forward! (Not Looking Back ...)

PHILIPPIANS 3:12-14

ALREADY PERFECT?

I love tearing open a special letter and poring through its pages, but almost more, I love listening as a letter is read aloud. And guess what? I get to listen as letters are read aloud every week in church. I especially enjoy the reader prefacing the letter like this, "From Paul's Letter to the Church in Philippi, we read..." I'm reminded that it's a personal letter, ultimately, from God to me. On one occasion, our vicar was reading the day's verses. This pastor-in-training was a great orator and boldly began proclaiming these words, only to immediately misread one of them without realizing his error. Vicar declared, "*Now* that I... am already perfect!" (With just one letter changed, the entire message was muddled!)

We laugh, then cringe, because we know we will not obtain perfection this side of heaven. Recall that Paul has been talking about sharing Jesus' resurrection power and His suffering. He knows that God is still at work in him, conforming him to Christ's death. He knows he has not yet obtained the resurrection because he is still in the race and running full speed with the Gospel. There is more work to be done; there are more souls to be won for Christ.

> Not that I have already obtained this or am already perfect, but I press on to make it my own, because Christ Jesus has made me His own. Brothers, I do not consider that I have made it my own. But one thing I do: forgetting what lies behind and straining forward to what lies ahead, I press on toward the goal for the prize of the upward call of God in Christ Jesus. (**Philippians 3:12–14**)

Paul likens his life in Christ to a race. **Chapter 3**'s run could be compared with **chapter 2**'s workout. There, Paul is exhorting the believers to exercise—live out—their God-given faith. Here, Paul gets more personal, as he admits his own humble efforts to continue relentlessly toward the day of Christ in His Savior's strength. To *press on*.

1. Again, Paul affectionately addresses the Philippians as "brothers" when he speaks about God's calling on his life and how he has not yet attained perfection. Why do you think he needed to tell his fellow believers this?

Run!

We often use "walk" to describe our Christian life. We are active in our walk of faith; we're given a path to follow; we have a goal . . . and a prize! "Because Paul's life was vigorous, he ran rather than walked. He labored because of his confidence in the Word of God" (*TLSB*, p. 2035). You and I persevere with the same confidence, straining forward with our eyes on the prize. And if our journey is a run, it's more a marathon than a sprint. God's call for us in Jesus is daily and lifelong. In Word and Sacrament, God gives us endurance for the long run. The run is "marked out for us" (**Hebrews 12:1** NIV) with a lane—a specific purpose and calling—all the way to the finish line.

2. While Paul doesn't use the word *run* in these verses, what words does he use that point to this kind of vigor and the imagery of running a race? Read **1 Corinthians 9:24–27** for another Pauline picture of the race he runs. How does it add to his explanation of his efforts? *Strains forward*
He beats his body to be his slave.
He preaches to others

3. *Prize* comes from the Greek word for *umpire*, the one who presents the prize at the end of the race (Lenski, p. 849). What is the prize for Christians? When do believers attain the prize? *Jesus.*
When they preach to others?

Special Delivery
Paul's first audience understood race imagery, as they were familiar with the foot races of ancient Greek influence, including the Olympics. A runner's perishable prize was a head wreath (or crown) of olive leaves or laurels (*TLSB*, p. 1959). The Christian's imperishable prize is the crown of eternal life (**2 Timothy 4:8**).

4. We know Paul remembers his past because he uses himself as an example (**Philippians 3:4–6**). Then what does he mean by "forgetting what lies behind" (**v. 13**)? What healthy reason could there be for recalling something that lies behind you? Have you struggled to let go of past failures or mistakes? When? Read **Psalm 103:12**. What does God say about your sins? *So great is His love for those*

our transgressions. who fear him that he has forgiven
as far as the east is from West

How easily Paul could have kept looking to his sordid past, but he leaves his wayward life behind; it is forgiven and done. If you've run, you know that looking back does at least two harmful things: (1) it slows you down, and (2) it distracts you by taking your eyes, even momentarily, off the finish line. The same is true in our faith walk. We don't rely on our past works or allow ourselves to be halted by past mistakes because we have His forgiveness for them. With God's help, we take any misplaced focus off the past so we can live (and run!) fully in the present.

STRAINING FORWARD TO WHAT LIES AHEAD

We can be excited about what lies ahead, knowing it involves God's calling for each of us and His continued work in us. First, God called us into the one true faith. Now and continually, "God draws us through His Word toward the way of life He intends for us, a life with purpose and meaning that endures" (*TLSB*, p. 2037). We are becoming more like Christ daily in our sanctification (spiritual growth, worked by the Holy Spirit).

In response to His call (**3:14**), chosen in the One who has made us His own (**3:12**), we *press on*, single-focused in our run, straining forward by His grace, motivated by the Gospel. He supplies all we need to finish the race. What lies ahead? Eternity with Christ!

CONFIDENCE, REVISITED

Our confidence in salvation and in the final resurrection lies in Christ's death and resurrection. My favorite quote from Dr. Jane Fryar follows: Paul stresses this, "not only as he thinks about the need to be justified . . . but also as he thinks about becoming more like Christ (**Philippians 3:12–14**). Whether we talk about justification or sanctification . . . we have no confidence in our flesh, our own effort and achievements. Our Lord justifies us by grace through faith. And He sanctifies us in that same way. He deserves and rightly receives all the glory" (*TLDB*, p. 1608). By His mighty power at work in us, we run, confidently proclaiming Christ.

Special Delivery
Paul's last known letter is 2 Timothy, written at the end of his final imprisonment from a Roman cell, where he faces imminent execution. Paul's final words on earth reveal his confidence in the fulfillment of Christ's promises. He has enabled Paul to remain faithful to the end. Paul obtained the prize, by God's grace: "The time of my departure has come. I have fought the good fight, I have finished the race, I have kept the faith. Henceforth there is laid up for me the crown of righteousness, which the Lord, the righteous judge, will award to me on that day" (**2 Timothy 4:6–8**).

JOYFUL Challenge: Think about this: you've been given a race, a lane, and a goal toward the finish line, where a prize awaits. God is giving you everything you need for the best run of your life. With God's help, what could serve as a catalyst to keep your eyes on the prize as you run?

Journal some ideas. Create a list of "my purpose" reminders as a go-to when you wane or stumble. (What has God given you to passionately pursue?) Seek accountability with someone you run beside, a sister in Christ or a Bible study group. Pace yourself with devotional time. Hold fast to His every Word, sister, remembering that He has made you His own. In Christ, you can press on!

Joy in Maturity

PHILIPPIANS 3:15-16

DEAR YOUNGER ME

In my junior year of high school, our English teacher gave our class heavy-duty notebooks and instructed us to write letters to ourselves daily all year. We were allowed to be as open and honest as we wanted with ourselves. That year especially, I struggled with confidence, identity, and self-image, and I dumped some of my struggles into the pages of my journal. Unfortunately, I wasn't looking to my Savior for help, strength, or healing, so my petty ideas of self-help and popular philosophy filled the pages instead. And they got me nowhere, but God eventually did.

It wasn't until years later that I recognized the immaturity of my faith in my younger years. On a visit to my parents' home, I found the notebook and was so upset by what I'd written years earlier that I threw it away. Now *that* incident was years ago, and I regret tossing the notebook in the trash. Only as I grew in God's Word could I discern between the world's petty ideas, "philosophy and empty deceit" (**Colossians 2:8**), and real help I receive from a real Savior, who gives me my identity, who trades my self-confidence for Christ-confidence, who says I'm beautiful. I'm still growing and maturing in my faith; you are too! We are a work in progress, but we trust He will carry His salvation work in us to completion on the day of Jesus' return (**Philippians 1:6**).

READING THE LETTER

Let those of us who are mature think this way, and if in anything you think otherwise, God will reveal that also to you. Only let us hold true to what we have attained. (**Philippians 3:15–16**)

Paul regards the Philippian believers inclusively, as he had in **verse 3** with "we are the circumcision, who worship by the spirit of God." Paul, a rock of maturity in the faith, implies that many of these brothers and sisters share the same maturity, and he exhorts all the believers to think this way and to act on it (to "hold true").

What is "this way," the way Paul tells us to think? Look back in **chapter 3**. This way is

☐ the way of righteousness by faith in Christ alone;

☐ the way of a runner, chosen and called by God for the race; and

☐ the way that means straining forward with eyes on the prize, confident in Christ and the salvation He has already won for them.

Thanks to Jesus' continual transformation work in us, we grow in maturity, and we may also think this way. "Maturity, then, comes by a life in the Word that strengthens the soul so it is dominant, overcoming the flesh" (Eschelbach, p. 610).

WHAT IF WE THINK OTHERWISE?

What if, even on some point, our thoughts are opposed to "this way" as Paul described in **chapter 3**? God will reveal that also to us. Do you find comfort in this? In our sin, our thoughts are easily swept in a wayward direction, especially as ideas and philosophies contrary to God's Word bombard us. Or when the evil one preys on our weaknesses, or when we fall for deceptive teachings that begin with God's truth but twist and pervert it. We need continual direction from God's Word. We may even find direction through godly people and in the circumstances God allows to teach us truth, clarify misunderstanding, and mature us. He brings us back from where we've strayed in our thoughts and lives.

1. "Also." One little word with so much weight. "God will reveal that *also* to you" (**3:15**). What beautiful truth does it imply? How did God reveal things to the believers?

HOLD TRUE TO WHAT YOU HAVE ATTAINED

What Paul says we have attained is "this way" (**v. 15**). Basically, this is where he gets to say, "Don't waver! Stand firm! Hold on tight to what you believe! Put into practice all you've received!" He knows that false teachers, like the Judaizers and any other Gospel-perverting group, will prey on the church. Paul

Special Delivery
Maturity = developed, Christlike character and behavior through a renewed mind (**Romans 12:2**) and tested faith; the goal for spiritual maturity is to be more like Christ. Spiritual growth toward maturity is a result of God's work through His Word.

Special Delivery
Consider this: the very words of this letter, personally delivered by Epaphroditus, are God's most recent revelations to the believers in Philippi, as God the Spirit inspired every one of Paul's words. The already-mature Christians would have opportunity for further growth and maturation of their faith.

is calling for a united front against all dangers and all attacks to the truth.

2. So much is packed into Paul's related words to the Colossians below. Circle the words that speak to our salvation—how we were justified or made right with God. Then underline our active response and the growth we have, by the Spirit's work in us (our daily sanctification). What's the danger? Mark a star by each word or phrase of warning, then write what you think each means.

> Therefore, as you received Christ Jesus the Lord, so walk in Him, rooted and built up in Him and established in the faith, just as you were taught, abounding in thanksgiving. See to it that no one takes you captive by philosophy and empty deceit, according to human tradition, according to the elemental spirits of the world, and not according to Christ. (**Colossians 2:6–8**)

3. I once fell for the pithy, supposedly Christian phrase, "God helps those who help themselves." God used other believers, in connection with His Word, to direct me away from this false thinking. The truth is, God helps those who cannot help—or save—themselves: sinners. Recall a time when you were immature in your thinking regarding your faith. How did God help you to see otherwise?

SPIRITUAL MATURITY

As we continue to mature in our faith, we take to heart the truth that we won't be perfected until the day of Christ but we are called to press for a Christlike life. We're confident He has made us His own, just as we're confident of His forgiveness and work in us. So we hold fast to the Word of life (**Philippians 2:16**), staying true to all we've attained, staying in the lane He's given us for the run of our lives.

4. Read **Ephesians 4:11–16** to learn more about spiritual maturity as a member of the Body of Christ. What role has the Lord given to pastors (shepherds) and other teachers of the faith? What's the purpose of equipping and teaching? What do they ward against? What does **verse 15** mean by "grow up"?

Grow up in the Body of Christ.

JOYFUL Challenge: What does someone say to you when you're behaving like a child? "Oh, grow up!" We know it's senseless to behave in a way that's contrary to the maturity we've attained through solid teaching, life experience, and other people's godly examples. While it appears, at times, that children are the only people exuding joy, there is JOY in maturity. How can you express that joy today?

☐ **Embrace** "what you have learned and have firmly believed" (**2 Timothy 3:14**) with confidence that you won't waver or wander when questioned or pressed about your faith.

☐ **Engage** with others in God's Word because there's always room to grow . . . and grow. (The minute I foolishly think I've attained greater maturity, I'm brought to my knees over an error in my thoughts or resulting actions. Praise God for His forgiveness and the chance to grow some more!)

☐ **Encourage** others who are growing in the faith, trusting God may use you as a mature example to them, one that's worthy of imitation.

Joy in Imitation

PHILIPPIANS 3:17

JUST LIKE YOU

Elizabeth has a "weekly appointment with God" that she set up several years ago and holds to this day. She meets with Him at her favorite coffee shop every Sunday before worship. She wrote to me, "I enjoy my time with God as I pray and reflect on my life, read Scripture, and write devotions. I look forward to it every week and have hardly missed an 'appointment.'" Periodically, Elizabeth would ask her college-age daughter if she was taking time to read the Bible and spend time with God. For a while, the answer was no. Her daughter was involved with a lot of activities and hadn't gotten into a routine yet. In her second semester, though, she wrote her mother a letter telling her how she started going to a coffee shop every Thursday morning before class just to spend time with God. She closed with "Just like you do, Mom" (*Raising Godly Girls*, p. 112).

Oh, that our lives would be worthy of imitation. Elizabeth's actions spoke even louder than words to her daughter, though she wisely chose words too. Like Paul, Elizabeth was humbly saying, "Join in imitating me."

Reading the Letter

> Brothers, join in imitating me, and keep your eyes on those who walk according to the example you have in us. (**Philippians 3:17**)

Joy is found in imitating those who imitate Christ. We can peek ahead to **4:9**, where Paul says, "What you have learned and received and heard and seen in me—practice these things." And to the Church in Corinth, he said, "Be imitators of me, as I am of Christ" (**1 Corinthians 11:1**). Paul also encourages them to look to others who are mature in faith. He is only one of many mature Christians who can serve as an example.

1. Find qualities worth imitating in the following verses—qualities that could be considered the marks of a mature Christian. Are there people in your life who exhibit one or more of these qualities?

   1 Thessalonians 1:6 *Imitators*

   2 Thessalonians 3:7–9 *Models*

   Hebrews 6:12 *imitate*

   Hebrews 13:7 *leaders, imitators.*

   3 John 1:11 *Imitators*

> **Special Delivery**
> "Joint imitators" is a most-direct translation in this verse, meaning, "all of you joined together in imitating me." The believers are not only to be imitators themselves but also to help and support one another in imitating Paul.

Imitating Imitated Imitators!

In Philippi, there were many who served as examples just like Paul. So consider this fun quote from biblical scholar R. C. H. Lenski: "Themselves active imitators, their very imitating is to be imitated, by each one of themselves as well as by all others" (Lenski, p. 857). Best. Quote. Ever. Isn't this what we desire to be and do?!

2. What's so important about having someone to look up to? Who has been or is now a godly example to you? How is that example valuable to you?

   I've learned the rights & wrongs.

3. Have you been someone's example to imitate, by God's grace? Do you know how your example has been valuable to them? Whose eyes are on you now, and what do you hope they'll imitate?

   My daughters, my faith

4. Is it possible that there is a danger in having an example to imitate? How can you protect yourself against this potential danger?

It's fascinating to notice the perfect placement of Paul's exhortations. He said earlier, in so many words, the Philippians should keep their eyes on Jesus, and he follows that with this plea to imitate those who imitate Jesus; to diligently look to their example. The believers are to stay focused because there are many disastrous examples to follow: enemies of the cross of Christ! So, to help the believers see the stark difference, he boldly contrasts the two, as we're about to see.

JOYFUL Challenge: Young children imitate their parents. That's perfectly normal and [usually] adorable. Motor and verbal skills are caught more than they are taught, and as each carefully imitated skill is mastered, the child's joy is impossible to miss. There's a special kind of joy that comes with imitating someone we trust and admire. When I'm watching someone walk with the Lord and see that he or she desires, above all things, to be more like Him—to love as He loves; to extend grace; to serve sacrificially—I am drawn closer. What about you? I asked you to think about someone you've kept your eyes on and want to imitate. What might that look like? Do you see that person serving in a way that interests you? Do you witness her treatment of others and want to have that kind of empathy? Do you relate to his passion for ministry and desire to go and do likewise? Imitate! And don't miss the joy that results.

Joy in Heavenly Citizenship

PHILIPPIANS 3:18-21

HEAVENLY THINGS

One of the most meaningful letters I've read was a memoir, often a biographical letter written to honor the memory of a loved one who's now with Jesus. Not long ago, my dear Pastor Paul went home to be with his Savior. Countless people came forward to share memoirs; they wrote letters to the family or posted them on social media, so all who knew him could learn about their memories with him, the many ways he touched their lives for Jesus, and the hope they have in Christ for a heavenly reunion. Pastor Paul's widow, Marian, said, "Although I'm grieving, I still have joy. Joy in knowing Paul's salvation. And though I continue to grieve, I know Christ's joy is mine too. Paul had no idea how many lives he touched or who would come forward and share their stories with me after his death." He pointed them to heaven, the place of our citizenship.

The memoir of someone who pointed others to Jesus points *us* to Jesus too. Such memoirs put our minds on heavenly things and away from the distractions of earthly things.

READING THE LETTER

> For many, of whom I have often told you and now tell you even with tears, walk as enemies of the cross of Christ. Their end is destruction, their god

Special Delivery
Who are the
enemies of the
cross of Christ? "In
particular, Jews who
refused to admit
their guilt under
the Law and so
refused to accept
that Jesus' accursed
death (crucifixion)
was really for their
sakes" (*TLSB*, p.
2037). In general,
those who deny
Christ, exhibiting the
shameful traits in
verse 19. Their end
is destruction. They
"die eternally, having
cut themselves off
from Christ, the
only source of life"
(Eschelbach, p. 611).

Special Delivery
Belly—This is a
general reference
to our sinful human
nature. Just as our
stomach signals us
that we are hungry
and bugs us until
it's fed, "so all the
desires of our flesh
tempt and nag at
us relentlessly until
we gratify them"
(Eschelbach, p. 611).
If the enemies' god
is their belly, their
"appetites" and
desires are entirely
self-centered
and even self-
destructive; their
glory in them is
their shame.

is their belly, and they glory in their shame, with minds set on earthly things. But our citizenship is in heaven, and from it we await a Savior, the Lord Jesus Christ, who will transform our lowly body to be like His glorious body, by the power that enables Him even to subject all things to Himself. (**Philippians 3:18–21**)

Here Paul employs a series of powerful contrasting statements concerning two people groups. **Verse 18** refers to one group as "enemies of the cross of Christ" and boldly describes them. In 4:1, he gives an encapsulating description for the second group: those who "stand firm thus in the Lord."

1. Two columns below outline the two groups Paul contrasts. Fill in the right column. Some of the answers won't be expressly stated here, so use the left column as your hint. What do these descriptions say about the measure of Paul's contrast and the urgency of his warning against the enemies of the cross?

Enemies of the Cross of Christ	Those Who Stand Firm in the Lord
Destruction (opposite of salvation)	*Salvation*
Self-centered (their god is their belly)	*Christ center*
Glory in shame	*Glory in God*
Earthly things (temporal things of this life)	*Heavenly things*

ENEMIES OF THE CROSS OF CHRIST

Paul is moved to tears over those who walk as enemies. He expresses his concern for the believers *and* his grief over the many who are not only lost but also leading others away from Christ. In 3:1, Paul says he's writing the same things to them as a safeguard; similarly, he reminds them here that he has told them often about these enemies. It's for their protection.

2. Compare our Philippians passage to **Colossians 3:1–2**. What is expressly stated in Colossians and implied by the contrast in Philippians? What is expressly stated in both, almost word for word? (Interestingly, one describes the enemies' minds and the other warns believers where *not* to set their minds!)

CITIZENSHIP

You've heard it said, be IN the world but not OF the world. Forgiven followers of Jesus, we are fully involved in the world, but not worldly—not OF it because we're really citizens of heaven, not of earth! (See **John 17:14-16**.) While we are privileged to be citizens of our country, complete with the freedoms we enjoy, we have an incomparably greater freedom in Christ, from sin and destruction. And He's returning to take us to the place of our forever citizenship.

FROM HEAVEN WE AWAIT A SAVIOR

Jesus is coming back for us. God's transforming work in us will be complete as He trades our lowly bodies for glorious bodies like Christ's. "Beloved, we are God's children now, and what we will be has not yet appeared; but we know that *when He appears* we shall be like Him, because we shall see Him as He is" (**1 John 3:2**, emphasis mine).

Special Delivery
The Philippians know all about citizenship; recall that Philippi is a colony of Rome, and many of the believers there had the privilege of Roman citizenship, a thing to be prized. Imagine how their ears perked to hear Paul talk about the privilege of a citizenship beyond compare.

3. What can we learn from **1 Corinthians 15:20-23, 42-44, 49-53** about this transformation that will take place at the final resurrection, when our divine Deliverer returns? How will He do this amazing work in us (**Philippians 3:21**)? *Since death come through a man, the resurrection comes through a man. By the power that enables him to bring everything under his control our bodies will be transformed into Christ bodies.*

4. What do you anticipate or look forward to the most about the day you'll see Jesus face-to-face? What do you learn from **Revelation 21:4**? *He will wipe our tears from our eyes. There will be no more death, mourning or crying or pain*

CAROL'S MEMOIR

Below is a memoir by my friend Carol in honor of her father. I pray you'll not only find comfort in her words, but that your mind and heart will be drawn heavenward to the place of your real citizenship.

This Friday marks the twenty-fourth year since my dad's passing. After losing my dad, I never thought I would be okay. His passing was so sudden. Who dies two weeks after being diagnosed with stage 4 pancreatic cancer? My dad.

Life kind of just slipped into autopilot then, as if the pause button on life had been pushed. Wedding plans were halted. Work and other activities were done in response to the need to do them, not the desire to do so.

Time hasn't healed my or my mom's or sisters' hearts. Jesus has. Jesus has provided healing through the kind and loving gestures of family and friends who have supported us. Through God's Word at just the right time with just the right message. We've grown deeper into our relationship with Him and have seen His promises fulfilled in a myriad of other ways in our lives.

I would give anything to have my dad back. To smell his Old Spice cologne. To see his bright smile and hear his sage and wise advice. . . . However, I wouldn't want to be without the healing love of Christ that sustains and encourages me each day. A love that softened the ragged edges of a broken heart and allowed a young girl . . . to live life again; profoundly altered, but full of hope and expectation. Dad and I will be together again someday. And it will be glorious and amazing because we will both be held in the arms of our loving Father of all eternity.

I think the healing process will never end. I'll always need support, encouragement, God's Word, a deepening relationship with Him, and reminders of His promises. And for this, I am grateful. Missing Dad but *rejoicing* in the many memories of time with him and a Savior who heals all wounds.

JOYFUL Challenge: The temptation is great—and constant—to fall into worldly living and priorities, a threat to our faith lives. We live in a culture of independence and individualism. We lack focus and discipline of godly pursuits. We are easily distracted by material comforts, worldly success, and vain appearances. When we feast on these, we starve our souls. Only the life, suffering, death, and resurrection of Jesus have the power to shift our focus; to save and nourish our souls.

List those earthly things—areas where you struggle the most with self-made "gods." Go ahead; courageously write them down. Then pray over them, laying them at the Lord's feet as you confess them to Him. Trust in His full and complete forgiveness for you at the cross of Christ. Praise Him for your heavenly citizenship. Rejoice that Jesus is preparing a place for you, and He will come back again to take you to be with Him forever. (Read Jesus' words in **John 14:2–3**.) Rejoice in knowing that one day you will be fully transformed and made perfect!

Joy in Standing Firm

PHILIPPIANS 4:1

The Sandwich Letter

Let me share a bit of fun advice you can employ the next time you need to impart some weighty words or important counsel to a loved one. "Sandwich" the meat of your message between warm, affirming, and encouraging words. Not only do these equally true words cushion the weight of your message, they also capture the attention and the heart of the reader. She's more likely to hear your warning well or respond proactively to your counsel.

Reading the Letter

> Therefore, my brothers, whom I love and long for, my joy and crown, stand firm thus in the Lord, my beloved. (**Philippians 4:1**)

Maybe you've noticed this "sandwiching" in Paul's joy-filled letter to his family in Christ in Philippi. Here in 4:1, as elsewhere, Paul precedes his instruction or warning with endearments, making clear his heart for these partners in the Gospel who are partakers with him in God's grace. Earlier he said he yearned for them with the affection of Christ; here he expresses his love for them and how he longs for them. Following his instruction, Paul gives one more shout-out to his friends before moving to a new topic.

1. Write the key words to the small sandwich that's tucked here in Paul's letter. What warm, endearing words precede and follow the exhortation—the "meat" of the sandwich? (It's no surprise that one term of endearment is "my joy"— don't miss this part of the sandwiching! ☺) And most important, what's the "meat"?

The Pauline sandwich of **Philippians 4:1**
Love,
My joy + crown
Stand firm

THEREFORE . . . STAND FIRM!

"Thus" is another way of saying "this is how to," a signal to look to the previous verses because they give purpose to this one. Paul wraps up this section of his letter with bold emphasis: *Stand firm* in your faith with your mind on heavenly things. *Stand firm*, not straying from the Gospel truth. *Stand firm* as you wait for Jesus' return. In a larger sandwich-sense, Paul has put a wealth of meaty counsel between his first call to stand firm (**1:27**) and this call to do the same.

Special Delivery
While a crown was commonly presented in honor of an accomplishment, Paul wasn't gathering jewels for a perishable crown, but souls for the crown of life (*TLSB*, p. 2037). This mention of a crown takes us back to **2:16**. He did not run in vain on their behalf. His crown is their enduring faith and salvation.

2. Look back to **3:12–21** and list every instruction Paul gives to help believers (then *and* now) to stand firm. Which of these instructions speaks loudest to you right now? Write it somewhere that you'll see it daily as a tangible reminder to seek God's strength and direction in this area. You could choose a note card, a sticky note, or a screen saver.

FACING OPPOSITION

Like Paul and like the Philippian believers, we take risks every time we stand firm, refusing to cave to the latest cultural craze that would have us wander from the truth. We are exposed to possible ridicule every time we share our faith. We come up against tidal-sized waves of opposition to or perversion of God's Word. Consider how Paul dealt with opposers and persecution. He exhorts all believers to do the same.

Special Delivery
In no other letter to a church does Paul speak so affectionately as he does to the Philippians. All at once, Paul expresses his love *for* them, his pride *in* them, and his joy *because* of them (Lenski, p. 865)!

3. How can we deal with ridicule, opposition, or persecution? After reading each point, personalize it to a situation you have endured or one that you or a loved one face now.

   ○ I can acknowledge the One who is in control, even when it seems the enemy has the upper hand. I can take it to God in prayer, trusting He has me (and the situation) in His grip. I can pray:

   Dear Lord you are in control,

❍ I can go immediately to the Word, where the Holy Spirit works powerfully to give me strength and direction. My go-to verse(s) will be:

Psalm 23

❍ I give God all the glory, confessing His Word and His work in all that I do as I stand firm and continue to confess Christ. I can say:

God have mercy on me.

Filled with the Holy Spirit, we depend on and trust in Christ's resurrection power at work in us, even (and especially) against what may feel like impossible odds.

4. What do the following verses have to say about the proactive measures you can take when you're up against opposition? Write these measures beside each reference and elaborate on what they mean.

2 Thessalonians 2:14–15   _Stand firm_

2 Timothy 4:3–5   _Keep your head in all situations endure hardships do the work of an evangelist_

Romans 12:2   _Be transformed by the renewing of your mind_

JOYFUL Challenge: I'll never forget an incident when I stood firm for the sake of my child; I took an unpopular position, and I was berated for it. Too often, I've backed down for fear of others and their opinions, but this time, in my Savior's strength, I didn't budge; to do so would have dishonored my Savior. (Please don't confuse this with belligerence or bullheadedness; I tried to cooperate but couldn't consent to a group decision because it went against my Christian values.) Later, I was overwhelmed with joy when an unexpected note appeared from my child: "I really admire the strong faith you have, and how you stand true to your morals, even when everyone around you doesn't. That inspires me so much, and I want to be like you."

Stand firm, sister! Not by bullheadedly planting your feet but by standing up for your Savior, His truth, and His children (of every age!) in a specific situation today or this week. What might this look like in your activities, commitments, or interactions? Whatever the outcome, you will overflow with joy, maybe even unexpectedly, as you trust and look to the One who enables you to stand firm.

Week 6
Group Study

☐ **Review every JOY Theme from this week.** Take turns sharing a portion or favorite question, along with your answers, from each study session, and discuss.

1. Joy in Pressing Forward! (Not Looking Back . . .)

2. Joy in Maturity

3. Joy in Imitation

4. Joy in Heavenly Citizenship

5. Joy in Standing Firm

☐ **Talk about your favorite JOYFUL Challenge.**

☐ **Share a JOY Snapshot.** See a general description in the Introduction.

Express JOY with a JOY ADVENTURE.

Are you ready for some adventure? As you recap this week's themes, consider some of the countless ways you might express your joy. For example:

☐ Sign up to run/walk a race for a cause. If you've never participated in a race before, let this give you eyes to see a finish line (as you press forward), a lane, a goal, and a prize! Word pictures do wonders to make us mindful of spiritual truths.

☐ Start a new ministry with a unique twist, employing your skills, passions, and growing maturity in your faith walk, and ask others to come on board with you to co-lead.

☐ Imitate someone you admire, stepping out of your comfort zone to go and do likewise. (I've had my eyes on a certain missionary; I'd love to join her in the field.)

☐ Write a memoir. (What a unique writing adventure!) Use it, in part, to point others to Jesus—to set their minds and yours on your heavenly citizenship.

☐ Take a risk as you stand firm in your faith. Ask a restaurant server, a store checker, or a complete stranger: "How can I pray for you today?" You may bring unexpected joy to their day, even as you live out an adventure.

Joy in Reconciliation

PHILIPPIANS 4:2-3

CONFLICT BETWEEN CHRISTIANS

I was overjoyed when God placed a woman in my path who shared my passion for a new ministry in our church. We worked side by side in preparation for the kickoff, and I treasured her wisdom and the mentor she was becoming. Then I said some pretty immature things while we were setting up. I was certain we should handle details a certain way, and she disagreed. I wouldn't back down; neither would she. When I wouldn't listen to her reasoning, she walked out the door. That put me in a panic. Would our conflict create an impasse? Would Satan use this disagreement to tromp all over a new ministry?

I was reminded of the reconciliation and healing that followed our dispute when I pulled out my prayer journal from that season of ministry. In it, I had written, "I praise You and thank You for answered prayer. You brought resolution to my conflict with [her] that had sent my nerves reeling. You gave me the words to write in a letter to her, and You gave me a reason to call her. Thank You." It was a difficult and humbling letter to write, but I realized my part in the conflict and humbly confessed it in an apology letter, recognizing that our blossoming friendship and ministry were incomparably more significant than our minor conflict.

> I entreat Euodia and I entreat Syntyche to agree in
> the Lord. Yes, I ask you also, true companion, help
> these women, who have labored side by side with
> me in the gospel together with Clement and the
> rest of my fellow workers, whose names are in the
> book of life. (**Philippians 4:2–3**)

Even when the conflict is minor, a clash between Christians serving side by side can negatively affect the entire Body of Christ and hinder the effectiveness of everyone's witness for their Savior. Paul has said much about unity already, and he knows that ongoing disagreements—much like envy, rivalry, and conceit (**1:15; 2:3**) —only breed disunity and factions; fellowship is strained by dispute.

1. Unity is always possible among believers because the Spirit is always present. Turn back to **Philippians 1:27** and **2:2**. What is Paul specifically urging the believers to have and do, by God's grace? How is that reflected here in this specific instance?

2. We know only what we read in these two verses about the disagreement between Euodia and Syntyche. Ponder the verses in detail and determine what we DO know, along with what's implied and what we can safely assume, based on all the information we have.

> **Special Delivery**
> "Euodia" and "Syntyche" were common names. In ancient writings, nearly twenty-five of each name has been found (Lenski, p. 866). Paul knew these two women personally and would have received acknowledgment of their disagreement through Epaphroditus when he came to Rome to assist Paul (**2:25**).

We can assume that the disagreement between Euodia and Syntyche has been going on for a long while. (It has reached the ears of Paul and he sees fit to address it, even as more time has passed since Epaphroditus brought this news to him.) Biblical scholars don't believe the disagreement was doctrinal in nature, or Paul would have addressed the topic specifically (Lenski, p. 867). Most likely, the two simply had differing ideas as they shared Gospel work.

THE BOOK OF LIFE

Paul cares so much for every individual in the church that he is willing to call out each of them by name, as necessary. He sees Euodia and Syntyche as partners in the Gospel, connected in their Savior to do His work. "The argument between ⌊them⌋ is noted, but of far greater importance is the fact that their names are written, together with all the redeemed, in the Book of Life" (Geisler, "For the Record").

Special Delivery

Book of Life—
Referenced at
least six times in
Revelation and
also by Luke, who
recorded Jesus'
words: "Rejoice that
your names are
written in heaven"
(**Luke 10:20**). It
has its roots in Old
Testament language
and reminds us of
keeping genealogical
records (Lenski, p.
872). It provides a
word picture for
the record of the
righteous, who will
inherit eternal life.

How much greater than Paul's Christlike love for the Philippians is the *perfect* love of the Savior for you and for me? We are individually known, loved, and cared for. God calls each of us by name (**Isaiah 43:1**). In fact, our names are written in the Book of Life too! He rebukes us in His Word, and He values us as His children. We partner with other children in His work; He is glorified and souls are won for Christ.

A MINISTRY OF RECONCILIATION

God reconciled us to Him through Christ, and now He's called us to a "ministry of reconciliation" (**2 Corinthians 5:18**), empowering us to reconcile people to Him and to each other, by His grace, and "entrusting to us the message of reconciliation" (**v. 19**). We've been reconciled so that we can reconcile. "We are ambassadors for Christ, God making His appeal through us" (**v. 20**). Sounds straightforward, but it can be so difficult to live out as we deal with broken relationships, broken homes, broken people, rifts, and arguments. And yet there is so much joy in reconciliation.

It can help to remember who and whose you are: a new creation in Christ (**2 Corinthians 5:17**). You're a precious child of God, cleansed, ransomed, and brought near to Him. In your own conflicts with others, *knowing your true identity and worth* can make all the difference in how you are able to treat them or handle the situation. With this focus, you can look at conflict in a new light as you ask yourself, "Who am I? A child of God, dearly loved. Who is the person I'm in conflict with? Also someone for whom Christ died."

3. Think of a time of conflict or disagreement with a friend. Pray, asking for God's strength to let go and seek reconciliation. Insert the same name(s) in each blank below and talk to the Lord. What can you do to spark and continue healthy communication in your friendships?

> God, help me to view myself and _____ as You view each of us. Forgive me for being critical of _____. _____ is Your chosen, redeemed child; give me patience and Your love for _____.

In Paul's Second Letter to Corinth, he makes an appeal to the believers.

4. Write out the words of Paul's appeal in **2 Corinthians 13:11** for some beautiful words of wisdom. With whom will you apply them this week?

JOYFUL Challenge: Seek reconciliation in His strength; become a peacemaker. This does not mean you can "fix" others. It means that because of the Holy Spirit, you can obey God by offering forgiveness. You can walk in humility, seeking to understand and listen. You can, "so far as it depends on you, live peaceably with all" (**Romans 12:18**). Take responsibility for your part, seeking to re-learn trust as you re-earn trust through faithful words and actions. And you can trust that God may use conflict in your closest relationships, bringing them through it to an even stronger place. He gives you the strength to not *retaliate* when you've been hurt, or *react* as the world does, but to *respond* according to His Word of truth; to respond as Christ would and according to His plan for reconciliation (**Matthew 18:15–17**). And by the way, there is so much *joy* in reconciliation, *joy* in laboring side by side for the Gospel with fellow believers, and *joy* in knowing your name is written in the Book of Life!

Joy in Relationship

PHILIPPIANS 4 : 4 - 5

JOY JOURNALING

Every healthy relationship requires good two-way communication. You write to me; I reply. You text me; I text back (with emojis). You call, "How soon can we meet for coffee talk?" I answer, "How about now?" God says, "I love you. I will fill you with joy!" in His Letter to me. And I write, "Lord, let me count the ways," in my letter back to Him.

My friend Karen Sue keeps a Joy Journal, mindfully recording the joys in her days, many of which would go unnoticed if not for her commitment to acknowledge them to the Lord. She calls them "happy dance" joy moments, and she recognizes at least one each day. Not only has this helped her during particularly rigorous seasons, but it has given her affirmation and peace during difficult decisions. "By writing down my 'happy dance' joy moments, I have a specific reminder of the joys I am blessed with each day. As I read over them, . . . I see how much good happens too. I know I can trust God and enjoy the blessings of the moment."

READING THE LETTER

> Rejoice in the Lord always; again I will say, rejoice.
> Let your reasonableness be known to everyone.
> The Lord is at hand. (**Philippians 4:4–5**)

There is so much joy in relationship! God speaks to us in His Word; we respond in praise and prayer or as we *joy journal*, like my friend! God designed us for relationship with Him *and* with one another. And in this passage, He refers to both. We enjoy relationship with the Lord, in whom we rejoice (**v. 4**). And we enjoy relationships with others; our reasonableness (gentleness and consideration) with them is evident (**v. 5**).

"REJOICE IN THE LORD ALWAYS..." -Phil. 4:4

MOMENTS of Joy JOURNAL

"Lord, Let me journal the ways!"

REJOICE! WHEN? *ALWAYS!* WHY DOES HE SAY IT AGAIN?

Remember that repetition in Scripture is as if God is saying "This is extra important!" Here, Paul doesn't just repeat it; he lets the reader *know* first. What a call to attention! We can rejoice in the Lord in every circumstance . . . even in persecution, even in suffering . . . even when reconciliation is necessary.

The Philippians can rejoice that they are reconciled with God through Christ and get to share that reconciliation with others. They rejoice as they serve their Savior side by side with purpose far greater than any dispute. They can rejoice that their names are written in the Book of Life. All of this is true for you and me—so let's rejoice!

JOY LIKE SUNSHINE!

One Bible scholar said it so well: "The purest, highest, truest joy is to fill the Christian life like sunshine . . . nothing is ever to dim our spiritual joy" (Lenski, p. 874). Paul is picturing "the life that is animated by the joy with which it shines . . . no matter what the circumstances of our life may be. Our sun of grace is '*always*' shining" (Lenski, pp. 874–75).

1. Does joy fill your life like sunshine? *Always?* What circumstances in recent past or now threaten to dim your joy? What promise(s) can you cling to when clouds of circumstances loom on the horizon? How could **John 1:5** and **Psalm 139:11–12** help?

JOY IN UNSTABLE CIRCUMSTANCES

In **1 Thessalonians 5:16, 18**, Paul says, "Rejoice always . . . give thanks in all circumstances." (*Joy* and *circumstances, always* and *all* in the same sentence. ☺) The JOY of Christ is ours by faith—always. No circumstance can strip us of this joy.

Author Donna Pyle said, "Sometimes we need to be reminded of God's stability in our unstable world. In His stability we find joy . . . regardless of our circumstances on any given day. We find that kind of joy only in the Lord" (p. 198). Because He is unchanging, we can trust in the stability of this relationship, regardless of our changing culture, job, health, even earthly relationships. Resting in our faith relationship with our Savior, we find unlimited joy. We can rejoice . . . always.

2. In what unstable or changing circumstances of your life have you most needed to know that the Lord is unchanging and perfectly stable, capable of providing rest in your relationship with Him? Did you recognize His presence or find joy in Him? Did you know you still possessed joy, despite your feelings? How will knowing this now make a difference in future circumstances?

Special Delivery
The Greek word here is *epieikeia*. The English translation *reasonableness* "expresses only a part of Paul's meaning; the Greek word that he uses points to . . . that largeness of heart, that spacious generosity, that freedom from the cruelly competitive scrabble of this world which only he possesses . . . who is heir to all that is Christ's" (*LBC*, vol. 2, p. 546).

REASONABLENESS → EVERYONE!

Relationship with the Lord, of first and greatest importance, makes all the difference in every other relationship. And here Paul moves from one to the next, immediately moving the believers to a Christlike consideration toward everyone. (Reasonableness could also be translated as thoughtfulness, gentleness, patience, generosity—a combination of all these and more.)

This Special Delivery contains a powerful quote, but how do we translate this into daily life, seeking to live out this expanded definition of reasonableness in all our relationships? Don't we want a large heart for others that's supremely generous and looks to others' needs ahead of our own? Don't we want freedom from that crazily competitive "me first" attitude?

The good news is we are freed by the Gospel to live like this. We know that our real citizenship is in heaven and we are co-heirs with Christ. God grant us the grace to be *reasonable* to everyone!

3. Write the names of three people with whom you share close relationships. How are you reasonable toward them? Where would you like to improve? What qualities do you most appreciate in them? How do these relationships bring you joy?

The Lord Is at Hand

Jesus is coming again! You can almost hear Paul shout with joy this final phrase: "The Lord is at hand!"

4. How does this eternal perspective impact all our relationships?

JOYFUL Challenge: Are you ready for a quick challenge you can do right now (and any time)? Consider the extent of JOY you have in your relationships. Point up to God, then to yourself as you meditate on His relationship with you: He sent His Son to save you and make you His own by His sacrifice at the cross. Point back up as you look up, lifting praise to God, fixing your eyes heavenward. Next, point from your far left to your far right, sweeping your arm horizontally, to remember all your earthly relationships, and thank God for them. You've just created the sign of the cross: the vertical beam, your relationship with the Lord; the horizontal beam, your relationship with others. Let this serve as a regular reminder that you can *rejoice* in every relationship.

Bonus: Read **Ephesians 5:19–21** for beautiful means of expressing His joy in all your relationships.

Special Delivery
Everyone?! Without exception? Yes! "Why should . . . even pagan persecutors be included? Many will not appreciate this [reasonableness]; but oh, the victories it has won among the worst enemies!" (Lenski, p. 875). Paul excludes no one when he writes "everyone."

Joy in Praying to the God of Peace

PHILIPPIANS 4:6-7

ANXIETY FREE

My daughter shares my predisposition toward anxiety. She shared with me, "Sometimes it hits me really hard and almost chokes me, like I'm so stressed out that I can't make myself get up and do anything about it."

One time, as a college student, she was feeling particularly anxious. In her devotion time, Courtney was reading Philippians, and that very night she was set to read **chapter 4**. She shared this in a letter to me later: "It was a total God-thing that I came across those verses on that day, and I knew He was trying to tell me something. I hadn't really prayed about it before, except with maybe a weak, 'God, I hate this anxiety.' So this time I prayed all-out."

Courtney unloaded everything that was weighing her down; each thing before the Lord, one at a time. Her letter continued, "And I don't know how soon it was afterward, but I realized that I felt free. All the weight of my anxiety was lifted off. God took it all away. I have never seen such a direct, tangible result of prayer before." Whenever the anxiety comes back (and unfortunately, it does), she prays about it just as she did then. And while she doesn't always feel the same degree of freedom and peace, she knows by God's grace that she has both (*Stepping Out*, pp. 62–63).

1.   What causes you anxiety? What are you often anxious about? (In the answer section, I've included a sizable compiled list of responses from a number of women.)

> Do not be anxious about anything, but in everything by prayer and supplication with thanksgiving let your requests be made known to God. And the peace of God, which surpasses all understanding, will guard your hearts and your minds in Christ Jesus. (**Philippians 4:6–7**)

Paul continues by acknowledging the believers' daily struggles and burdens. He addresses what can happen as a result: anxiety. Paul, of all people, knows struggle firsthand. He would have every reason to be anxious! After all, the verdict is still out: will he be freed? further detained? executed? Only the Lord knows, and Paul's life is in His hands. So are the Philippians' lives. So are yours and mine.

2. What does Paul say there is to be anxious about? _____! The apostle Peter calls out anxiety too: "[Cast] all your anxieties on Him, because He cares for you" (1 **Peter 5:7**). (If they're cast on Him, they're no longer yours.) That said, do you think there is a place for legitimate concern, as opposed to anxiety? If so, give an example.

Notice Paul does not tell us to "just try harder" to be at peace. But God does have a plan for us. He speaks through Paul to give us (A) instructions and (B) a promise.

(A) God's instructions for us = PRAYER—His antidote for our anxiety.

3. What should we bring to the Lord in prayer? _____. What do **Isaiah 65:24** and **Matthew 6:8** tell us about God's knowledge, concerning our prayers to Him? Why should we pray about everything that we're anxious about? Does God answer every prayer?

God tells us to come to Him with every request; His beautiful instructions also tell us how:

☐   **By Prayer and Supplication:** At His invitation, we come to God with *everything*. We confess our sins; we make supplications (petitions, requests) for ourselves and others; we lay in His hands every anxious thought, from the smallest to the largest.

☐ **With Thanksgiving:** Every request is made from this perspective. We *acknowledge* what He has done and how He answers prayers. We *praise* Him for salvation and for the hope we have in Christ. We *thank* Him for taking care of every need and anxiety we lay before Him now, even though we don't know what the outcome will be. Regardless, we trust His will and His work through each request, by His grace!

(B) God's promise to us = PEACE

Our sins are forgiven. The peace of God is *peace with God*—we are reconciled with God in Christ. (See **Colossians 1:19–20** and **Romans 5:1**.) Peace is in the tranquility we receive as we give all our cares to God and no longer cling to them. He imparts this peace in us by the Holy Spirit.

GOD'S PEACE SURPASSES ALL UNDERSTANDING

"Surpasses all understanding" is often misinterpreted. It does not mean God's peace is beyond our comprehension entirely. (We *do* know the sweetness of His peace by faith.) It actually means this is the peace that surpasses what the mind alone is capable of doing, regarding our thoughts and our hearts. Believers don't have to rely on their minds in a vain attempt to ward off anxiety, as worldly people do when they seek only secular answers to manage the mind and purge anxiety (Lenski, p. 879). Here, Paul points to something that far surpasses the mind's limitations: God's peace that He imparts on us as a gift in Christ Jesus. We may not fully understand it (**1 Corinthians 13:12**), but we receive it freely. Jesus said, "Peace I leave with you; My peace I give to you. Not as the world gives do I give to you. Let not your hearts be troubled, neither let them be afraid" (**John 14:27**).

His peace guards our inmost thoughts and our faith in Christ Jesus. We may wonder how He can promise peace when life makes no sense, but we have His Word on it! In our own strength or mindful attempts to combat anxiety, we try to "hold down the fort" alone, but we're poor defenders at best. Yet His peace stands over our hearts and minds, and nothing can disturb them. The peace of God surpasses all else! He can give peace in the most difficult circumstances. And while they may not change, by His grace we do.

4. When have you unexpectedly experienced peace? The kind of peace that would lead an unbelieving world to say, "There's no way she could have peace in the middle of that!"

JOYFUL Challenge: Pray about the anxieties in your life right now. Thank God for taking care of these anxieties, even as you don't yet know how He will do that or what it will look like. Lay every care in His hands. Remember: you are praying to the God of peace. Rejoice! His peace is standing guard over you. Even when life makes little sense and your mind can't reason or understand peace, you can "Trust in the Lord with all your heart, and do not lean on your own understanding. In all your ways acknowledge Him, and He will make straight your paths" (**Proverbs 3:5–6**).

Write down one anxiety and place it by your Bible or near a cross or other visual faith reminder. As you tangibly let it go and leave it there, trust that God is taking your anxiety from you and replacing it with His peace in Christ. Try this again tomorrow...

Joy in "Whatever!" (All That Is Worthy of Praise!)

PHILIPPIANS 4:8

THE PERFECT SENTIMENT

Oh, for life to be like greeting cards! Not that every thought and every conversation would sound like a Hallmark card, with rhyming couplets or canned sentiment. But consider all the reasons for sending cards and letters. From celebratory milestones to words of encouragement to shared suffering—and everything in-between. We choose just the right card and put the utmost care into every thought before we pen our greeting. We say only things that build up the recipient. We wisely choose honorable, lovely sentiments for the good of the recipient.

How different life could be if we gave the same careful thought toward others in every situation. Are our thoughts as true as those we penned in our letter? Are our intentions pure, as when we sent a card out of love or sympathy? I'll admit, I don't always park my brain in the healthiest places. So I take my less-than-true thoughts to the Lord and confess them to Him. In His grace, He leads me to park somewhere worthy of praise.

1. Where do you park your brain? Could you use a little time in the sentimental section of the card shop? Pause now to confess your less-than-true thoughts to the Lord, trusting in His full and free forgiveness.

> Finally, brothers, whatever is true, whatever is honorable, whatever is just, whatever is pure, whatever is lovely, whatever is commendable, if there is any excellence, if there is anything worthy of praise, think about these things. (**Philippians 4:8**)

Even more poetic than the sentiment of a card are the words of today's verse, rhythmically flowing from **verse 7**. Here, we see the primary virtues of a heart and mind guarded by the peace of God in Christ Jesus. A mind fixed on *whatever* is worthy of praise!

The virtues Paul lists are the "fundamental ideals of life according to God's design" (*TLSB*, p. 2038). It's no wonder Paul stresses that we continually "think about these things" because the influence of our thoughts on *all* of life is tremendous. All that fills and occupies our minds will be evident in our words and actions, directing everything we do. Of course, the Holy Spirit produces these God-pleasing thoughts in us, powerfully working through the Word.

2. As a unique way to help define these fundamental ideals we're to fix our thoughts on, find words or phrases with the opposite meanings (as a caution against letting our minds wander). Use a dictionary or Google as necessary.

True—

Honorable (Noble)—

Just (Right)—

Pure—

Lovely—

Commendable (Admirable)—

Excellent—

Worthy of Praise—

Special Delivery

Whatever—One word, written and repeated five times in this verse, stresses the same thing: anything and everything and only such that is true, honorable, and so on. Recognize its purposeful repetition, emphasizing each virtue or ideal, encouraging the reader to pause and consider them one at a time.

THINK ABOUT THESE THINGS

Our English word "think" falls short. "These things" are not just nice goals for our thought life. We are to meditate on them for what they are, and not substitute or stray away from them. With God's help, we can fix our thoughts on these things.

3. Look at each value or ideal. Bring it close to home by giving specific examples from your life. For instance, God's creation in nature is *lovely*; God's Word is *true*; an honest day's work is *commendable*. Additionally, think about one person in your life and ask yourself, "What about this person is honorable? just? of excellence?"

4. When these values are at the forefront of your mind, how can they help you "take every thought captive to obey Christ" (**2 Corinthians 10:5**)?

DOWN IN MY HEART

Let's have a little fun thinking about some of "these things." First, do you have *the joy, joy, joy, joy down in your heart*? YES! You've got it because He put it there . . . to stay! It's *true*! You have been chosen by God in Christ, covered in His *purity* and righteousness, and by faith, you possess this joy (whether you're currently feeling full of joy or not). Isn't that *lovely*? Christ has gifted you with salvation, purchased for you by His death and secured for you in His resurrection. (Nothing could be of greater *excellence*!) The Holy Spirit has taken up residence in your heart; you are filled with the Spirit's power (and fruit), and He is at work in you. He is always *worthy of praise*!

JOYFUL Challenge: Let's revisit joy moments. They happen in hugs, laughter, a good meal, a warm blanket, the first sip of a favorite beverage, a kind word, and more! They happen in a favorite place (go there, at least in your mind, and see it in detail with new eyes). They happen when you delight in a detail of God's handiwork. They happen in all kinds of ways and places and through all sorts of means. In the happening of any of these joy moments, ask yourself, "What about this is true or honorable, lovely or excellent?" Think on these things and rejoice. Thank God for them. And share your joy . . . in the moment . . . and again and again!

Joy in Living Out What We've Learned

PHILIPPIANS 4:9

PUT IT INTO PRACTICE

My friend Kelly wrote this letter about a young woman who put into practice something that is true, lovely, and commendable. Clearly, the young woman had learned it in her own life, and it flowed in her words and actions. Kelly's letter challenged me. Do I put into practice what I've learned?

> Tonight as I was sitting outside Starbucks waiting for my friend, two college-aged girls walked by. One of them walked back toward me and said, "You look nice today. I just want you to know that." I mumbled "thank you," and tears filled my eyes. What she did not know is that hours before, I had looked in my mirror and criticized everything about my look: my hair was too flat and my scalp showed no matter how much hair spray I used. I hoped my concealer would hide my blemishes. And I spent the whole car ride debating whether I should eat dinner because I don't need any more calories. Her kind words brought hope and love to my weary soul. May I be more like her . . . may we all be like her. Be genuine, show kindness and love, and let's lift each other up!

Only God knew the insecurities and struggles Kelly faced that day, and He used a lovely young woman to speak truth to Kelly's heart. Her actions were truly commendable. May we put into practice whatever we've learned—whatever is true, lovely, commendable, and more, from the Word of truth and from every Christlike, positive example in our lives.

READING THE LETTER

> What you have learned and received and heard and seen in me—practice these things, and the God of peace will be with you. (**Philippians 4:9**)

If ever there were two verses suited for each other, it is yesterday's and today's. Yet each deserves its own study for all that is packed into them and all the reasons for joy found in each. From "think about these things" (**v. 8**) to "practice these things" (**v. 9**)—from thoughts to action! Believers are called to action, to let all their "minding" take root and blossom; to produce fruit in their lives by the Holy Spirit's power.

Special Delivery
"What you have . . ." In some translations, NIV for example, this phrase is another "whatever"! Regardless, it intentionally flows forward from **verse 8**'s list of values, pointing the reader right back to them.

1. Write four distinct ways the Philippian believers have received "whatever is true." Based on what you know about Paul and the Philippians, write examples of how, when, or through what means they have benefitted and grown in these ways. Jot them beside each of the first four verbs from today's verse.

    1. _____

    2. _____

    3. _____

    4. _____

THOUGHTS → WORDS → ACTIONS → LIFE

The believers knew that Paul lived what he believed and taught; he could say: "Join in imitating me" (**3:17**).

2. Our thoughts inspire and influence our words, our lives, and all we do.

    Thoughts → Words → Actions → Life

    Expound on an example of this chain reaction in your own life. How has one led you to another, and another (for good or bad)?

3. In the Colossians verses below, circle the word we saw six times yesterday and similarly today in our Philippians verses. Does "everything" really mean everything or only things connected to our faith life? List all you learn about "whatever" in these verses. How and where can you practice these things too?

> And whatever you do, in word or deed, do everything in the name of the Lord Jesus, giving thanks to God the Father through Him. . . . Whatever you do, work heartily, as for the Lord and not for men, knowing that from the Lord you will receive the inheritance as your reward. You are serving the Lord Christ. (**Colossians 3:17, 23–24**)

4. As we put our "whatevers" into practice, God gives us a promise, also in **verse 9**. We could say it's a twofold promise, as we look at **Romans 15:33** and **2 Corinthians 13:11b** for similar promises. What are they? What does this mean for us? *Love & Peace*

LIVING OUT WHAT WE'VE LEARNED

Several years ago, my then-five-year-old and I were finishing his usual bedtime scenario. Prayers were said, the Bible story had been read, and the race to bed had begun. I purposely held back, as I always did, making certain he would win the race. Cameron flew down the hall, around the corner, and disappeared into his room to crawl under the covers. "Mom, try to find me!" came the familiar singsong phrase. I began my routine. "Let's see, where could my boy be? Is he in the closet? No. Behind the door? Not there either. Hmm. Where is Cameron?" This time though, instead of my usual, "There he is!" and tickle attack, I said, "I give up. It's just impossible." Silence. No wiggles or giggles under the covers. Then a quiet, serious reply: "Mom, all things are possible with God."

My son's words brought me *joy*! He was able to share what he knew, to live out what he'd learned. He knew the *truth*. I was right there with him. He trusted I would find him and wrap my arms around him with tickles and love. Even more, he and I both know the greater *truth*: the Lord seeks us and finds us. Jesus' *pure* and perfect sacrifice for our sins assures us we are forgiven—we have peace with God, and He is with us. He chooses each of us as His own dear child and wraps His love around us—nothing could be *lovelier*. All things—even the salvation of sinners like you and me—are possible with God in Christ Jesus (see **Mark 10:27**). And that, my sisters, is most *excellent and worthy of praise*!

JOYFUL Challenge: Recall Kelly's story. Have you been the recipient of unexpected kindness or generosity from someone who is joyfully practicing what they've seen in a godly example? They're literally *living out* what they've learned and received for themselves. Write about one or more of your own stories. Then be on the lookout for ways you can bring joy to others as you live out truth, honor, justice, purity, love, and more ... practicing what you've received!

Week 7
Group Study

☐ **Review every JOY Theme from this week.** Take turns sharing a portion or favorite question, along with your answers, from each study session, and discuss.

1. Joy in Reconciliation

2. Joy in Relationship

3. Joy in Praying to the God of Peace

4. Joy in "Whatever!" (All That Is Worthy of Praise!)

5. Joy in Living Out What We've Learned

☐ **Talk about your favorite JOYFUL Challenge.**

☐ **Share a JOY Snapshot.** See a general description in the Introduction.

Express JOY with JOY GIFTS.

Share your *joy in relationship* with a few special people in your life by giving each of them a gift. Maybe you've recently reconciled with a loved one over previous conflict. Surprise that person with a visit, talk time, and dessert—your treat. Maybe a co-worker or classmate could use a pick-me-up: stop by with a bouquet of flowers. Is a sister-in-Christ anxious about a decision or a health crisis? Put together a prayer basket and deliver it to her, offering to pray with her too. Maybe a young family just had a baby: take them a meal, along with disposable dishes for quick cleanup. Has a friend needed a break? Present her with movie tickets and a box of candy. Is a senior sister lonely? Give her the gift of your time, and create a craft or complete a puzzle together. The options for gift-giving are as broad as your relationships are varied. With every gift, express your joy, share of yourself, and show them Christ!

Start here

Joy in Knowing the Secret!

PHILIPPIANS 4:10-13

SECRETS REVEALED

Secrets are hard to keep to yourself, right? Knowing a secret means you have information that maybe only you are privy to. How exciting! And when you get to share or celebrate the secret— even better! I'll never forget some of the letters I've received that revealed secrets of the best kind.

Years ago, I was part of a "secret sister" group. All year, my "sister" sent me letters, Scripture-rich notes, and small gifts of encouragement; they continued coming in the mail, even after my family moved away midway through the year. God worked through her provision to bring me peace and strength (and yes, joy!) through a rigorous year filled with change. At last, Christmas came, and she revealed the secret of her identity. I finally knew who had prayed for me and encouraged me anonymously all year long. Knowing this secret brought even greater joy as I gave thanks to God for her!

When my husband was at the seminary, we received a handful of letters containing generous gifts from supporters who wished to keep their identity a secret. Their generosity was coupled with the truth that the real Source of our provision, the Secret to contentment in our new life as a student family, was Christ! Although we didn't know their identity, we knew the Secret, and we still share and celebrate this Best. Secret. Ever!

> I rejoiced in the Lord greatly that now at length you have revived your concern for me. You were indeed concerned for me, but you had no opportunity. Not that I am speaking of being in need, for I have learned in whatever situation I am to be content. I know how to be brought low, and I know how to abound. In any and every circumstance, I have learned the secret of facing plenty and hunger, abundance and need. I can do all things through Him who strengthens me. (**Philippians 4:10–13**)

Rejoice Greatly!

Paul again rejoices over the Philippians in his last mention of joy in the letter. He emphasizes his joy with *greatly*, which shows how delighted he was when this generous, loving gift was so unexpectedly presented to him by Epaphroditus and his joint messengers from Philippi.

1. Why does Paul *greatly rejoice* in the Lord over them? In what ways is the Gospel's work in their lives evident?

"The delay in sending gifts to Paul was not the fault of the Philippians, nor was it because they were lacking in concern for him" (*CSSB*, p. 1822). They have always had Paul on their hearts, but difficult times had hit them and sent them into severe poverty for several years, which had not improved until recently. Just as soon as they could, they gave what had been on their hearts and minds to give all along (Lenski, pp. 887–88).

Content WHATEVER the Circumstances

Paul's words make it clear that his contentment is not determined by or dependent upon earthly possessions. "In whatever situation I am . . ." Paul could be discontented—even disgruntled or distraught—but instead he is able to see the blessings in every one of his situations, trusting God to use them for good (remember **Romans 8:28**?), provide for all his needs, and be glorified through them.

2. What two extremes does Paul contrast by a threefold mention of them? Write the words or phrases he uses to describe each. Why do you think he mentions times of "plenty"? Aren't people naturally content when they lack nothing? What's the issue with that, and what does it say to us today?

One extreme: _Abound_, _plenty_, _abundance_

The other: _brought low_, _hunger_, _need_

As Paul moves from "plenty and hunger" to "abundance and need" in **verse 12**, he moves from the specific (food) to the general (all human and bodily needs). Consider his use of repetition again, and the purposeful progression emphasizing his contentment in *all* situations.

THE SOURCE AND SECRET

Paul knows the secret; he celebrates and shares it with every reader! The source and secret is CHRIST—His strength in us because we are united with Him.

Special Delivery
Content (Greek *autarkes*) can mean having sufficiency, independent of external circumstances. Paul's sufficiency is from his Lord.

Author and former missionary Elisabeth Elliot wrote, "The secret is Christ in me, not me in a different set of circumstances" (Smith).

☐ *Christ in me*, giving me strength for every new and potentially difficult situation.

☐ *Christ in me*, giving me contentment in all circumstances.

☐ *Christ in me*, filling me with His joy, peace, and power.

3. Read more about Christ's power and strength FOR you and IN you. Make notes and personalize these verses for your life in Christ.

2 Corinthians 12:9–10 _For when I am weak, then I'm strong._

Ephesians 3:16–17 _He may strengthen you with the power of the Holy Spirit in your inner being_

Colossians 1:11 _Being strengthened with all power according to His glorious might so that you have endurance patience joy_

Poverty is just one of many burdens for Paul and for the Philippians; they need strength for many reasons, and they receive it continually from the One who empowers.

Just because you may not know how God is working in your circumstance doesn't mean He doesn't. Trust that He is always at work, and He can change *you* even if the circumstance doesn't change. Trust Him to strengthen you *for* it and *in* it. No situation can rob you of God's promises to you or His joy and strength in you. As He fills you spiritually, you can be content in every other way: physically, mentally, and emotionally. Find your contentment in Him.

4.   Write what it means for you, personally, that you can do all things through Christ who gives you strength.

SHE KNOWS THE SECRET

My friend Kelly knows the secret:

> I learned the true meaning of joy when, at the age of 22, I was diagnosed with stage 3C ovarian cancer. Before surgery, the doctors said, "We may need to take all your reproductive organs." After surgery, they told me, "You have six months to live." My happy, smiling, and laughing self vanished with these words. Sadness, tears, and anger filled the holes. Yet in the weeks following, I felt peace deep down inside of me. I was at peace with my circumstances. . . . I realized that even though the cancer had taken over my physical body, it could not take over my spirit. My God was bigger than the cancer, and that knowledge gave me joy. Others around me could sense this peace and joy within me. They could not understand how I could be joyous in my circumstances of dying, vomiting, and exhaustion. They knew joy only as the world knows it. The world's definition of joy is being happy and careless. Cancer taught me that joy is much deeper than what the world thinks it is. Joy is a fruit of the Spirit. It is being *content* regardless of the circumstances. I knew I could die from this disease. However, regardless of the outcome, I could live knowing that Jesus already defeated cancer and my eternal death. Even if cancer overtook my body, it could not overtake my soul. God loves me so much that He sent His Son to die for me. Cancer could take my health, my hair, even my smile, but it was not strong enough to take away the power of Jesus and the salvation I have in Him—and that is true joy.

Praise Jesus, the source and secret to Kelly's peace, contentment, and eternal joy! Over ten years later, she's a walking miracle!

JOYFUL Challenge: "[Paul] knows how it feels to be cold and hungry. Still, he lives in joy. This is not a 'paste a smile on your face and pretend to be happy' joy. And it's not an 'I always feel good' joy. It's a joy that keeps on going despite outward circumstances and inward feelings. It's a joy that explodes in hearts that trust our Savior's promise that nothing can separate us from the love of God in Jesus and His cross" (*CCBH*, p. 398). (See **Romans 8:39**.) Paul has this joy because he knows the source and secret to his strength, joy, and contentment in every circumstance.

You know the secret too! May it give you the same joy, exploding in your heart because you believe your Savior's promise: nothing can separate you from His love. He is your strength. Reread your answer to Question 4. How can you share this, your secret, today?

Joy in Generous Living and Sacrificial Giving

PHILIPPIANS 4:14-18

GIVING TO THOSE WHO GO!

Our nephew Jace traveled to Puerto Rico as part of a mission team and sent a letter to thank us for our support and tell about his team's service. Everything had impacted him greatly, from teaching Bible school to the native children to assisting with the rebuilding of a home destroyed by a hurricane. Jace closed by thanking us again for our prayers and support. He added, "My trip to Puerto Rico was a well-needed energizer for my walk with God too."

It's humbling for my husband and me to hear that God used our prayers and our gift to help with Jace's Gospel work in another part of the world. We couldn't go, but we could support someone who *could*! We were anxious to hear from him and to thank God with him—to *rejoice greatly*—for the work done in Jesus' name. Jace could share the burdens of those he met and ministered to, and in a sense, so could we through our support. I pray that Jace's offering and ours were both gifts "acceptable and pleasing to God" (4:18).

READING THE LETTER

Yet it was kind of you to share my trouble. And you Philippians yourselves know that in the beginning of the gospel, when I left Macedonia, no church entered into partnership with me in giving and receiving, except you only. Even in Thessalonica you sent me help for my needs once and again. Not that I seek the gift, but I seek the fruit that increases to your credit. I have received full payment, and more. I am well supplied, having received from Epaphroditus the gifts you sent, a fragrant offering, a sacrifice acceptable and pleasing to God. (**Philippians 4:14–18**)

The Philippians share Paul's burdens every way they can. They pray for Paul; they sent help in Epaphroditus; they sent physical aid, giving generously out of their poverty. Their tangible gift reveals just how deeply they care for him.

1. Paul talks about what their generous gift means to him. As we see in **verses 14 and 18**, Paul sincerely appreciates their gift, but he is not ultimately dependent on it (*CSSB*, p. 1822). His joy in this gift is not for himself, but for them. Why? What does their gift reveal?

IN THE BEGINNING OF THE GOSPEL

From the time Paul left Philippi after founding the church (**Acts 16**), they've supported him, providing for his needs. Their generosity is unmatched by any other. Christ's love flows through the believers in Philippi. They had been emboldened to trust God to meet their needs, which freed them to generously give to Paul for the sake of the Gospel.

2. Read **2 Corinthians 8:1–5**, where Paul is talking about the Church in Philippi (and the others in Macedonia) to the Church in Corinth. Write out some of his descriptive words concerning the extent of their hardship and the measure of their generosity. How do we know they gave freely?

    By the depths of their faith, their devotion to the Lord

FRAGRANT OFFERING

The *fragrant offering* was rich in meaning with the history of God's people. Paul would have known it well and shared it as he taught. According to Old Testament laws, priests had to repeatedly offer sacrifices to God on behalf of the people. The spilled blood of animals was to cover the people's sins. The sacrifices were burned on the altar, and the smoke of the offerings would rise toward heaven, "with a pleasing aroma to the LORD" (**Leviticus 1:9, 13, 17**). This may not sound fragrant to us, but it pleased God because the sacrifices were offered in sincere faith and repentance, and God provided forgiveness through them. But because the sacrifices were imperfect and incomplete, regular offerings were required.

When Jesus offered His life as the final, perfect, and complete sacrifice to the Lord, He fulfilled the Old Testament laws once and for all, fully covering the sins of all people for all time. His was a sweet sacrifice for our sakes, a fragrant offering, perfectly pleasing to God. (See **Hebrews 10:1–18**.) By His grace, we are able to present our bodies "as a living sacrifice, holy and acceptable to God" (see **Romans 12:1**), living our lives for Him.

3. Why could the Philippians' gift to Paul be received and celebrated? In two more letters to churches, Paul talks about *fragrance* or *fragrant offerings*. Who or what does he reference in these verses: **Ephesians 5:2** and **2 Corinthians 2:14–15**? How do all these fragrances tie together?

Those who are saved.
Christ is the ultimate fragrance

Special Delivery
Thessalonica is also in Macedonia, only about a hundred miles from Philippi, and was Paul's next stop on his second missionary journey (**Acts 17:1–9**). Although itself an infant church, Philippi sent Paul support gifts almost immediately after his departure: *Even in Thessalonica, and not just once but twice!* No other church ever partnered with Paul in this way.

"It's God's Intervention"

My friend Elizabeth recalls the move-in after her husband received his first call as a church worker.

> Fresh out of college, our little family of four moved from Minnesota to Iowa. Taking our first position at a church, we didn't have much since we had pared down to go to school full time. When we arrived at our cute little farmhouse rental, Ruth greeted us with toys for our children, food for breakfast, and encouraging words for us. She walked around our house, making a mental list of what we would need and said, "I'll be back!" Wow, was she ever "back" for the rest of the years we lived in Iowa. She loved to shop at garage sales, and she would show up, time and again, with just what we needed. I was amazed at her timing, and she always said, "It's God's intervention." She truly was the messenger God sent to meet our needs "according to His riches in glory in Christ Jesus" (**Philippians 4:19**).

Ruth's generous offerings were fragrant, indeed! God's provision through even one of His people is heartening and helpful in our faith walk. We thank Him for every prompting, for every act of generosity, as He uses His children to meet the needs of others and draw us closer to Him.

4. Think about a time when you were on the giving or receiving end of a fragrant offering, the means through which God provided, to meet a need and to bless His people. Was there a special connection between you and the giver or recipient, and did it develop further? How does it feel to give? to receive? Why is it important to do *both* graciously?

JOYFUL Challenge: Who has been an example or role model for you? Think of someone who doesn't cling to material blessings but recognizes that as they've been given, so they want to give. They live with open, extended hands. They may even go without so someone else can receive. Now that's *generous living and sacrificial giving*! And there's so much joy to be found in it, as God leads us to it and provides both the means and the heart for it. How can you imitate what you've seen in this kind of example? Where do you feel a nudge to give? Prayerfully consider, then commit to one specific person or ministry and present your own aromatic offering to God.

Joy in God's Rich Supply

PHILIPPIANS 4:19-20

GREAT PROVIDERS

When I hear *Father* and *supply*, I think of my dad and mom, who are great providers. Growing up, I never wanted for anything. On our family farm, my parents raised cattle, crops, chickens, a garden, and three girls. ☺ Our farmhouse sat amid ranchland and farm ground, and even in years of drought, we never went without. In fact, we had all we needed and more. My parents were as warm and generous as they were hardworking.

One of the greatest gifts my parents gave during our growing years was that we rarely missed church, busy as we were on the farm. My dad replaced his sweat-stained cap with a straw or felt Stetson (depending on the season) every Sunday morning. During service, he always had pens in his shirt pocket, and if I began to get unruly, he would hand one to me. I felt great comfort leaning into Dad's big arm or Mom's soft shoulder. Sometimes I fell asleep during the sermon to the feel of Dad's western-cut suit against my face. He and Mom listened with quiet reverence to the Scriptures and knelt humbly at the altar for the Lord's Supper.

As my parents led me to my heavenly Father's house, I am reminded of the gentle way my Lord leads me each day in my walk with Him. I still come into His presence like a child, and when I begin to get unruly, He quietly redirects me through His Word and gives me forgiveness through His Son's sacrifice in the Sacrament. Ultimately, He is the great Provider; He supplies all that I need . . . and I praise Him for the provision that came through my parents too.

READING THE LETTER

> And my God will supply every need of yours according to His riches in glory in Christ Jesus. To our God and Father be glory forever and ever. Amen. (**Philippians 4:19–20**)

The Philippians have supplied Paul beautifully, and he *rejoices greatly*! Now he lets them know that they, too, will have a beautiful, rich supply for every one of their needs, according to God's glory in Christ. (See also **Ephesians 1:18**; **3:16–20** for more about the riches of God's glory.)

Remember that they've been struck with poverty, opposition, and other hardships. From love and concern, Paul shares God's promised provision. He is blessed to receive their gift, which is a sacrifice, an offering, pleasing to God (**Philippians 4:18**) (Lenski, p. 897).

OUR NEEDS

In our sin, we seek after the wrong things, attempting to satisfy ourselves with substitutes for needs only God can fulfill. And guess what? We're left lacking. That's because *no one else* and *nothing else* can give what we need most: grace in Christ, peace, joy, contentment, satisfaction, and more. God, our Father and Provider, knows our needs (**Matthew 6:31–33**), and He takes care of *every* need, even as He uses His people to tangibly meet some of them. His riches in Christ, which far exceed our earthly riches, would have us live today in light of eternity. "All the riches of God become available to us because of what Christ did" (*TLSB*, p. 2039) for us.

1. Write down every need you can think of, whether it's physical, material, emotional, or spiritual.

   a. Which items are basic, tangible needs on a given day? Which are emotional? spiritual? (Label basic needs with B; emotional needs with E; spiritual needs with S.) Look at the list again and highlight those which, when fulfilled, give you joy. (It's okay if food gives you joy; it's one of God's good gifts, after all.)

food
shelter
Clothes
Nice things

Special Delivery
God's promise of provision is not restricted to only the provision of our heavenly eternal future with Christ, though it is certainly the pinnacle! His provision refers also to our present life, to every need we have here and now. (In **verse 16**, Paul mentions his needs of this life, and now he refers to the believers' similar needs.) Although Paul cannot supply those needs, God can and will (Lenski, p. 897).

b.   Do any of your needs distract your view of the prize and the finish line? Pray about all your needs, asking God to reveal which ones aren't healthy or aren't needs at all. (Some "wants" are good things; others distract.) God often provides generously beyond our needs! Finally, look at every healthy need and thank God because He is ultimately the provider of them, as He knows best. Trust Him.

Love, family, grandchildren, Friends, God, Church, Faith

NAILED IT!

Christian bumper-sticker-esque quotes, church marquees, and one-liner social media posts are everywhere. Most don't stick with me, but one did. It said: I NEED JESUS. Whoever posted this nailed it. Every other need faded as I thought about the one thing I need.

2.   How can Jesus be your only need? Share your thoughts, then share a faith-based one-liner that stuck with you too.

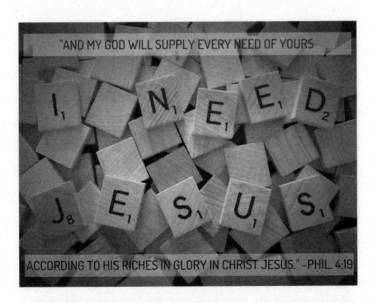

"AND MY GOD WILL SUPPLY EVERY NEED OF YOURS

I NEED

JESUS

ACCORDING TO HIS RICHES IN GLORY IN CHRIST JESUS." -PHIL. 4:19

Compelled to share the same one-liner, I created my own graphic. Try designing one that stuck with you.

OUR GOD AND FATHER

Paul refers to believers as "children of God" in **Philippians 2:15** when he says we "shine as lights in the world." And we've read the endearing words of **1 John 3:1**, reminding us of the Father's love "that we should be called children of God."

3. We referenced the following verses previously, but let's take a closer look. Rejoice in the reasons you can call God your *Father*, as Paul does here. *Circle* "children of God" in both passages below. Then *underline* the reasons why you're a child of God. Finally, *highlight* every relationship word (like *Father*). How does it feel to know the God of the universe created you, calls you by name, and adopted you as His precious child, by whom you cry, "Abba—Daddy!"?

I feel special

> But to all who did receive Him, who believed in His name, He gave the right to become children of God, who were born, not of blood nor of the will of the flesh nor of the will of man, but of God. (**John 1:12–13**)

> You have received the Spirit of adoption as sons, by whom we cry, "Abba! Father!" The Spirit Himself bears witness with our spirit that we are children of God, and if children, then heirs—heirs of God and fellow heirs with Christ. (**Romans 8:15–17**)

GLORY!

After penning **verse 19**, Paul breaks out in praise! Perhaps as he considers the truth of what he's written by the Spirit of God, he can no longer contain himself. You can almost hear him shout, "To our God and Father be glory forever and ever. Amen."

4. God, by His perfect nature, is eternally and completely full of glory. What can we add? Yet we glorify Him in our lives. In **Philippians 3**, Paul said we "glory in Christ Jesus" (**v. 3**) but unbelievers "glory in their shame" (**v. 19**). Turn back to **Philippians 1:11** and **2:11**. How do believers give God glory? How is He glorified in your life today? What does "glorifying God" look like *any* time in *any* place? (Think in terms of your daily walk.)

We produce the Spirit's fruit in our lives. By being thankful

JOYFUL Challenge: Breathe in; then slowly exhale. (Go ahead . . .) God just gave you another breath, another moment of life. Rejoice! Look back upon the past several days. Recall the kind *clerk*, the camaraderie of *loved ones*, your favorite *foods*. Reflect on the changing *seasons*, God's daily *provision* of specific needs, and above all, the *faith* He has instilled in you to know that Jesus is Lord and He is risen. God is the Great Provider in every circumstance you face today and for every need you'll ever have, both physical and spiritual. Rejoice in His rich supply. With newly opened eyes, look at *one specific thing today* that you've been given. Gaze at it with thanksgiving *for* it and joy *in* it. Your heavenly Father is the Giver of "every good and perfect gift" (**James 1:17**). Rejoice!

Joy in Greeting Fellow Believers in Christ

PHILIPPIANS 4:21-22

GREETING EVERY SAINT

Writing a sermon can be like writing a letter. It often begins with a warm greeting, includes a story, and contains at least one important message. It points people to Jesus, shares truth and love, and so on. Okay, maybe this is an oversimplification. Most of my letters aren't as profound as my husband's Law-and-Gospel sermons, though sometimes they pack a punch. Always included in both, however, is the warm greeting I mentioned. Sometimes Cory begins his sermon with "Dear brothers and sisters in Christ," or he quotes Paul with, "Grace to you and peace from God our Father and the Lord Jesus Christ" (**Philippians 1:2**). Cory begins as though he's sharing a letter, if you will, from God's Word and from his own heart, to the hearts of the listeners. He is greeting every saint in Christ Jesus.

READING THE LETTER

> Greet every saint in Christ Jesus. The brothers who are with me greet you. All the saints greet you, especially those of Caesar's household. (Philippians 4:21-22)

These are Paul's final greetings. He wants to make sure the recipients of his letter share these warm greetings with one another, with every believer—saint—in Philippi. Paul's words in 1:1

made clear that he writes "to all the saints." The whole church is to hear the letter read publicly.

All of Paul's companions—Gospel workers with him in Rome—send greetings too. This would have included Timothy, for sure (see **1:1** and **2:19–24**). "Such greetings broadened and deepened the relationships between congregations and between leaders" (*LBC*, vol. 2, p. 415).

Consider the brotherly affection behind Paul's request to "greet," written three times in two verses. I love the translation "embrace" because it's a tangible expression of Christian love between people as they give and receive the peace and love of Christ. In many letters, I've written "when you see them, give them a hug from me!" In effect, this is what Paul writes to the believers: "Embrace one another on my behalf, and on behalf of the brothers and sisters here too."

1. At the close of Paul's letter to the Romans, following a long list of personal greetings, he expresses the warmth with which all the believers are to greet one another. Read **Romans 16:16**. What is it? (See also **1 Corinthians 16:20; 2 Corinthians 13:12; 1 Thessalonians 5:26;** and **1 Peter 5:14**.) Why might this common request seem uncomfortable for some congregations and Christians today?

   Greet one another with a holy kiss

SAINTS IN CAESAR'S HOUSEHOLD

These greetings from the believers in Rome include "especially," Paul says, "those of Caesar's household" (**Philippians 4:22**). These people are "not blood relatives of the emperor, but those employed (slaves or freedmen) in or around the palace area" (*CSSB*, p. 1823).

Many believers of Caesar's household were already members of the original congregation in Rome prior to Paul's arrival. It's intriguing to consider, however, that some are followers of Jesus as a direct result of Paul's detainment. They've been drawn to Christ through Paul's life, witness, and words. Paul has undoubtedly developed relationships with those who are in close proximity to him; the Holy Spirit has worked powerfully as he boldly shared the Word of God! We can assume Paul has regular interactions with them, especially now that his trial is going before the imperial court.

2. As Christians who serve under the tyrannical Caesar Nero, why might the members of Caesar's household be grateful for their proximity to Paul and interested in the outcome of his trial?

We can imagine how fondly Paul has spoken to the saints in Caesar's household about his beloved friends in Philippi, since they are asking him to include greetings from them in his letter. Maybe some of them have even attended to Epaphroditus during his grave illness. Again, we are reminded of God's work—advancing the kingdom and saving souls—through Paul's imprisonment.

GREETINGS!

3. Let's look at a few places in Scripture where we read of *greetings*. Describe the greeting in each of these passages. Who gave the greeting, where, and why? How was it received? Look for JOY connected to every event.

Luke 1:26–38, 46–47 *The angel gave the greeting to Mary. It was received with Faith*

Luke 1:39–45 *Mary greeted Elizabeth. Luke with joy*

Matthew 28:1, 5–10 *The angel, at the tomb, with joy*

COMING BACK

My friend Elizabeth knows the great value of a greeting. She shared:

A lot of teasing goes on about where you sit in church. Someday I am going to make a name plate for "my spot." Joking aside, it proves we are creatures of habit. In my family's former church, "my spot" was two rows from the front on the left side. On one particular morning, I saw a new couple seated behind me. I offered my hand and said, "Hi! I'm Elizabeth." They had come to see a co-worker sing in the praise team that day and had no intention of coming back. But soon, there they were again. Creatures of habit that we were, we were in "our spots" every Sunday, greeting and talking. They began coming to my house for Bible study, then became very involved in our church.

Special Delivery
Prominent in the original Roman congregation are the imperial servants and slaves. There were two groups of these slaves belonging to Nero, the current emperor. These slaves were highly educated men who managed finances and estates, and they were often more capable and intelligent than their owners (Lenski, p. 899). (See **Romans 16**.)

the spirit rejoice in God

We've known each other nearly sixteen years now and have stayed in contact even after my family moved away. They attribute coming back each week to a warm greeting, but I know the truth: it was God's plan all along.

What starts as a simple greeting can become an extension of God's love through us and His plan to use us . . . and who wouldn't want to keep coming back?

4. How do you typically greet brothers and sisters in Christ when you meet for worship and at the start or closing of a service? Do you, in some manner, share the peace of Christ? How may your simple greeting cause someone to keep coming back?

JOYFUL Challenge: How important is the greeting one believer gives to another? Whom will you get to greet *with joy* this week? How will you share Jesus' peace? Often, what you do depends upon the culture of your family and church, your comfort zone, and how you express His peace and love to others. This week, get out of your comfort zone! Maybe that means stepping into the aisle where you greet someone new (or someone new to you). Introduce yourself; offer a hand or a hug. And extend your greetings beyond the church service. Visit someone you haven't seen for a while. Greet someone special with the warmth and affection that reveals their value to you and their worth in Christ.

Joy in God's Grace for Us in Christ

PHILIPPIANS 4:23

GOD'S GRACE BE WITH YOU . . .

When I write thank-you cards, I'm overcome with warm feelings for each person and search for just the right words to express how much the gift meant and, even more, how much the giver means to me. And I love to close with words of grace and joy. God has graciously given to me through their generosity, and I pray that His grace flows out of me and onto them. So I close, "God's grace be with you. Joyfully yours, Deb."

READING THE LETTER

The grace of the Lord Jesus Christ be with your spirit. (**Philippians 4:23**)

Paul opened his Letter to the Philippians with a warm greeting and blessing: "Grace to you and peace from God our Father and the Lord Jesus Christ" (1:2).

1. Compare Paul's words in 1:2 with his benediction and blessing at the close. What beautiful words overlap? What rich messages does Paul proclaim in either or both blessings over all believers who hear or read, as the blessings bookend the letter?

   Grace, the Lord Jesus Christ

WE NEED HIS GRACE!

In a few of my favorite devotions by Dr. Dale A. Meyer, I am reminded just how completely dependent I am on God's grace. He writes, "The good things we do aren't enough to save us and never will be enough. That includes our religious works like going to church, doing devotions, contributing to church and charities, and so on. You just can't pile up enough merits to climb into heaven, can't work your way out of the hole of guilt. Only God's forgiveness and kindness in Jesus Christ saves us, only grace. . . . Forgiveness is grace and salvation a gift, not the result of your work. . . . Ultimately we are dependent upon our loving God for His help" (Meyer, p. 324). "Total and complete help [comes] from our divine Helper. Some people give lip service to grace but really don't think they need help. How about you? . . . Lord, . . . lead us all to acknowledge our need for Your grace in Jesus Christ. Amen!" (Meyer, p. 288). "By grace you have been saved through faith. And this is not your own doing; it is the gift of God, not a result of works" (**Ephesians 2:8–9**).

Grace is at the heart of our relationship with the Lord and at the center of our salvation. "It is grace . . . that brings people into a relationship with Him and keeps them in that relationship until they go to be with Him forever. . . . From that grace flow all others blessings, such as peace (4:7) and joy (4:4)" (Gernant Dumit, p. 62).

2. Because of God's first gift of grace, and out of His great love for us, we receive countless other gifts. A couple of these gifts have been named for you: peace and joy. Below are a few more. As you study the sampling below, provide a brief definition or explanation of each one, based on what you know of these gifts already and using the verses provided. Ponder each gift and the difference it makes in your life, received *and* shared. What other God-given gifts come to mind?

   Contentment from receiving all blessings shelter, food, family love

Special Delivery

Grace = unmerited, undeserved saving favor of God! By His grace, we receive His forgiveness for our sins. We receive faith by the Holy Spirit—salvation for our souls. We inherit eternal life and look forward to a bodily resurrection. We have God's grace, the greatest blessing we could receive in Christ!

Special Delivery

With your spirit—Not just one part of a person, but the whole person, as seen from the inside, the core of his or her being (*CSSB*, p. 1823). (See also **Galatians 6:18** and **2 Timothy 4:22**.) This is not to be confused with the Holy Spirit, the Third Person of the Trinity, who lives in us and through whom we believe.

Faith—Acts 16:31; Romans 5:1; Galatians 2:20

Hope—1 Timothy 1:1; 1 Peter 1:3

Comfort—2 Corinthians 1:3-4

OVERFLOWING GRACE

"The grace of our Lord overflowed for me with the faith and love that are in Christ Jesus" (1 **Timothy** 1:14). When God fills us to overflowing with His grace, He is speaking of plenty, abundance, and being "beyond measure." Envision the overflowing splash of God's grace onto those near you. Maybe they'll be drenched in it because it has poured out of you in great quantities, *by God's grace*. One Philippians commentary said it well: "The grace of the Lord Jesus is so abundant that it flows over from Paul to us through this very Word and has the power to overflow from our lives into the lives of others, so that we genuinely . . . extend God's grace to them" (*LBC*, vol. 2, p. 547).

3. Extending (splashing!) God's grace to others means giving them what He first gave us: favor and forgiveness, even though they don't deserve it and can't earn it. (That's the point.) Who comes to mind as you picture the splash, the overflow, of God's grace pouring out of you and onto them?

GOD LEANED IN

A very dear friend shared with me a time when God gave her opportunity to extend grace. It wasn't easy. It rarely is. She wrote, "I was handed an armload of harshness and words that didn't make sense to me, but God leaned in at that moment and reminded me what extending His grace meant. I knew it meant lowering my voice, stating facts, apologizing if necessary, and allowing His grace to fill the gap between us."

God's grace flowed through my friend in such a welcomed way! She could have reacted with the same harshness she had received, but *God leaned in*. She continued, "We don't know the shoes other people walk in; we usually only think of our own. God's grace is a place we can walk into, relax, and breathe as we soak up His comfort and peace." It's a place we can take others to, as well.

4. When have you been handed an armload of harshness or callous, critical words? What can you do that will help you remember *God leans in* just when you need His strength the most, enabling you to respond graciously? Does it also help to consider the other person's situation—that he or she is another person for whom Christ died?

JOYFUL Challenge: For your final daily challenge, I've chosen something fun: acronyms! Here are a few to get you started. Your challenge is to create your own acronyms. Save them, share them, post them, and use them as reminders and definers of the incredible JOY you have in God's GRACE for you in Christ—the GOSPEL! Others to try: REJOICE, MERCY, LIFE, LOVE, or PEACE.

☐ **JOY** = **J**esus **O**ccupying **Y**ou!

☐ **GRACE** = **G**od's **R**iches at **C**hrist's **E**xpense

☐ **GOSPEL** (Try a sentence acronym) =

God created us to be with Him.

Our sins separate us from God.

Sins cannot be removed by good works.

Paying the price for our sin, Jesus died and rose again.

Everyone who believes in Him has eternal life.

Life with Jesus starts now and lasts forever.

Week 8
Group Study

☐ **Review every JOY Theme from this week.** Take turns sharing a portion or favorite question, along with your answers, from each study session, and discuss.

1. Joy in Knowing the Secret!

2. Joy in Generous Living and Sacrificial Giving

3. Joy in God's Rich Supply

4. Joy in Greeting Fellow Believers in Christ

5. Joy in God's Grace for Us in Christ

☐ **Talk about your favorite JOYFUL Challenge.**

☐ **Share a JOY Snapshot.** See a general description in the Introduction.

Express JOY with a JOY BOX.

Find a medium-size box with a lift-off or flip-up lid. Purchase a pretty one, ready to use, or pick out a plain one that's ready to paint, decorate, or decoupage. (If you're planning ahead for group time, maybe you'll make plans to personalize your boxes together.) Somewhere on your box or inside the lid, write your name and "JOY BOX" (or something similar ☺).

Make a sticky-note list to tuck near your box or under the lid to remind you what to put in your JOY BOX.

Start your list while seated next to your sisters in Christ, as you wrap up your group study time, mindful of this final week's topics and reasons for rejoicing. What kinds of tangible mementos and small reminders will you tuck in your box? Secret notes? Small gifts from a generous friend? Reminders of God's rich supply? How will your box give you a giggle or a smile, especially on those I-don't-feel-one-bit-joyful days? I pray it may provide proof that you have many blessings and reasons to *joy dance, joy sing, joy talk,* and ultimately, rejoice in your Savior!

Need more ideas for your box? A small *joy creation* you made earlier, a memento from a *joy adventure*, greeting cards, love notes, ticket stubs, Scripture cards, photos, inspirational quotes, song lyrics, event programs, travel souvenirs, letters from loved ones, encouraging words from your study group, and more!

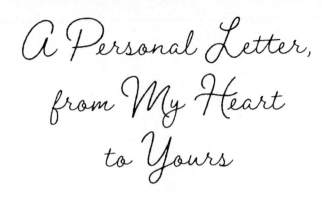

A Personal Letter, from My Heart to Yours

My dear sister in Christ,

I thank God for you, and I pray that you are rejoicing now! I also pray that you have grown in God's Word through this time in Philippians. Let me challenge you one more time by asking this: How do you hope, in your Savior's strength, to continue growing in your walk with Christ?

As with every cherished letter, this one has come to its close. But because it is a love letter that is ultimately from God's heart to you, keep it close and read it over and over, rejoicing in His timeless message of grace to you in Christ.

All joy is ultimately from the hand of God, and because His hand is always upon you, reasons to rejoice can always be found. So rejoice, first and foremost, in God's free gift of salvation in Jesus, His Son and your Savior! As the Holy Spirit nurtures this precious fruit of JOY, may it burst forth as evidence of the faith that fills you and permeates your life. Because true joy resides deep within your soul . . . because it's grounded in the unshakable faith that's yours in Christ, you can live with the same humility, confidence, and contentment Paul describes throughout his letter. You are a work in progress, growing in faith and joy. In the day of Christ's return, your joy will be perfected, complete, and eternal. Daily, ask the Holy Spirit to fill you with the joy of the Lord. By His grace, may you always look to Him, the secret and source of all your needs.

Paul's repeated reminders to *rejoice in the Lord* express his joy and the joy he hopes to ignite in his readers, by the Spirit's might. I believe he could have paused at any point and proclaimed, "I rejoice! Do you rejoice?"

I pray *you* rejoice in Jesus today, my friend. God's grace and peace to you in Christ!

I am *joyfully yours*,
Deb

A Thank-You Letter

This book has been a work in progress for several years now, on some level. Every time I travel to lead a retreat, digging into Philippians with new friends and sisters in Christ, I walk away joy dancing! Sisters, you know who you are: *thank you* for "retreating" with me to the Letter of Joy. You listened and learned, shared and encouraged; you provided invaluable input and inspiration!

Thank you, Cory, my God-fearing husband and the spiritual leader of our home (and theological guide too!). You've been my sounding board and hand holder throughout this special (and rigorous) time. Your clever gift from my favorite chocolatier has been a yummy incentive: a joy-indulgence, savored one-per-day as the words flowed. Love you bunches!

"You've got this, Mom!" I cannot *thank you* enough, Chris, Courtney, Aaron, Cameron, and Katherine, for your prayers, texts, and words of love that have kept me going on this joy journey. You shine His light so brightly!

To my parents, Dick and Gene, my sister Connie, and in memory of my sister Lisa. *Thank you* for showing me Jesus; for loving me JOYfully through thick and thin; for your faithful prayers and continual support!

More than thirty friends and loved ones have contributed to this work, sharing stories, quotes, or life with me. *Thank you* for infusing joy into this work and into my life, and for allowing me to use your stories and share your hearts. ☺ Still others sat with me over coffee, prayed with me, or helped me giggle, sing, and joy dance. Some of you spoke to me with gut-level honesty or soothed me with your words, face-to-face and from far away . . . *thank you*.

I've been blessed with the most amazing team at CPH: Peggy, Elizabeth, Laura, Holli, Lindsey, Alex, and others! *Thank you* for your support and encouragement, editing expertise, marketing marvels, and stellar graphic design skills. And *thank you*, Shelly, for your words of encouragement, along with your personal edits from the home front!

Above all, I *thank God* for all of you: "Always in every prayer of mine for you all, making my prayer with joy, because of your partnership in the gospel" (**Philippians 1:4–5**).

Joyfully yours in Jesus,
Deb

Daily Study Session Answers

WEEK 1

DAY 1

1a. They had just endured false accusations, beatings, unjust—even illegal—imprisonment, and torture in stocks. In a response that defied logic, Paul and Silas prayed and sang hymns to God. After the earthquake broke their bonds, they remained and saved the jailer from killing himself. They were calm in the face of chaos; they rejoiced in the midst of their suffering with praise and prayer, confident of their salvation and God's plan for them. They believed God was using them as His instruments.

1b. Yes, the other prisoners; the jailer and his family. We know the other prisoners were listening as Paul and Silas lifted their voices in praise and prayer, and when everyone's bonds were broken in the earthquake, they could have fled but they didn't. What a powerful testimony the missionaries' worship was to all who listened, especially the jailer, who had just witnessed the unthinkable: no one escaped, though they could have; they stayed to spare his life!

2. Responses will vary. If your reaction revealed only your pain, take it and every struggle to God in prayer; rest in His grace and seek His strength that enables you to move forward with forgiveness.

3. Responses will be unique, but may include "Believe in the Lord Jesus" (**Acts 16:31**), God's Son, sent to take your sins from you. He defeated death at the cross, dying in your place as punishment for your sins and rising victoriously, saving you! This belief—faith—is yours by God's grace, given freely out of His love for you, undeserved and unearned, but yours because of Jesus!

4. Through service; he washed their wounds and gave them bodily nourishment. Ultimately, he expressed faith when "he rejoiced along with his entire household that he had believed in God" (**Acts 16:34**).

DAY 2

1. Answers will vary. Consider each possible recipient and words that define her well.

2. We are saved by God's grace, His forgiveness and favor that we cannot earn and don't deserve but freely receive because He loves us! Our faith is a gift of God, through no work of our own. We are made right with God by this gift of grace, through Christ's redeeming work in our place on the cross—for you and me! No gift could be greater than the FREE gift of eternal life in Jesus! And all of God's other gifts are ours too, *by His grace* through faith.

3. God works peace into our lives and hearts by the power of the Holy Spirit; peace (like joy) is a fruit of the Spirit, which is produced in our lives by faith. Jesus tells His followers in **John 14** that the peace He gives is unlike anything the world attempts to provide. We have perfect peace with the Father through Christ, who reconciled us to Him; we receive eternal peace through the salvation won for us at Christ's cross.

4. Answers will vary.

DAY 3

1. He rejoices because of their reception of the Gospel by faith and for their partnership with him in the spread of the Gospel.

2. Their hearts were full, and they gave in response, generously and joyfully. Even when Paul was in Thessalonica, they sent generous help/support for his needs. They gave sacrificially out of their poverty to help in the relief of other believers too.

3. Responses may include these: It's freeing to give, to know that this support is, in part, enabling a person or ministry to thrive in serving and sharing the Gospel. Relationships grow among us. Encouragement is given and received.

4. Answers will vary.

DAY 4

1. Christ's love for us is an abiding love; it's a love that endures, is steadfast and unshakable. He loves us with the same unconditional, eternal love the Father has for Him. He loved us enough to sacrifice His life for us.

2. Our love for our friends imitates Christ's love for us, by His grace! Everything we do can be done in abiding, even sacrificial, love for our friends. Answers for ideas to enrich friendships may include give them your time; show them preference; listen well; live authentically beside them; show and give them grace; pray for and with them.

3. The path of life—the way, the truth, and the life—IS Christ (**John 14:6**)! God has made the way to eternal life known to us: faith in Christ, by His grace. By faith, He lives in us; in His presence, there is not only joy but the fullness of it . . . for eternity!

4. Joy moment stories will be unique to each person.

DAY 5

1. Filled with *knowledge* and *discernment*.

2. By faith, we are made right with God (righteous) and produce good fruit in our lives by the Holy Spirit. Filled with Christ's righteousness, we are able to love as He does. We can discern truth according to His Word. We're made "pure and blameless" in Him, by grace through faith.

3. Wording will vary; God desires that we abound and continue to grow in love for one another, filled with the knowledge of His will. He works in us, enabling us to do these things and filling us with the knowledge of His will for spiritual wisdom and understanding.

4a. With the truth of God's Word tucked securely in our minds and hearts, we can face questions of direction or purpose with certainty and clarity of God's will. Filled with truth, we won't fall for false teachings or the lies of Satan. By God's grace, we can speak the truth in love (**Ephesians 4:15**)—loving as God first loved us: unconditionally and sacrificially.

4b. The ultimate purpose of living righteous lives by faith in Christ is to glorify God by our words, our witness, and our very lives. "Pure and blameless" is not without sin, but rather covered in Christ's purity and blamelessness. We're covered in His pure robe of righteousness (**Isaiah 61:10; Romans 3:22**) and blameless only because He took our blame from us at the cross (**Colossians 1:22**).

WEEK 2

DAY 1

1. Answers may include scary, uncertain, lonely, unbearable, harsh, unjust, persecuted. Paul is self-forgetful; his focus is not on the state of his circumstances but on the advancement of the Gospel. He is looking upward, not inward.

2. Everyone around him knows that he is NOT in chains for committing a crime, but for spreading the Gospel of Christ.

3. Paul is talking about the Gospel of Jesus that he preaches when he says "for which I am suffering, bound with chains as a criminal" (**2 Timothy 2:9**). The Word of God is not bound!

4. Maybe you were treated unfairly or cruelly; maybe you've been through scary times involving a loved one, work, finances, or health issues; maybe you're going through a difficult time in a relationship. While we may not have all the answers now, and might not even have them until heaven, we can trust in our Lord today that there IS a reason. He is the ultimate Help, hanging on to us, even when we can't get a grip.

DAY 2

1. (1) From envy, rivalry, and selfish ambition; to afflict Paul while he's imprisoned (thinking their own success would make Paul envious of them). (2) From good will and love, knowing Paul is imprisoned because of his defense of the Gospel; desiring, all the more, to courageously share it!

2. Paul rejoices because Christ is still preached in truth and purity, regardless of motives. He is unaffected by their competitive rivalry or envy; the spread of the Gospel is all that matters.

3. Stories will vary. Even if we have reason to believe motives are selfish or tainted, we can openly respond, like Paul, with joy because God's truth is shared. We should examine our own feelings and attitudes; maybe (like the jealous proclaimers) we struggle with envy over others' opportunities or success. What matters is that God is glorified in their service and ours; only He knows our hearts. It may also help to listen to them and get to know them better, recognizing their unique contributions.

4. His attitude toward the two camps doesn't differ at all. To see so many believers speaking out so courageously makes Paul rejoice! He won't allow their motives to squelch his joy. He can respond selflessly with no resentment. "What then?" is as if to say "What does it matter?" Who cares about the motive when the truth is shared and souls are saved for Christ?!

DAY 3

1a. Paul is certain that this will result in his deliverance, no matter the result of the trial. Paul says he *knows* this *will* turn out (not just that he *hopes* this *may* turn out). Because Paul *knows*, he can face his future with confidence and joy!

1b. (1) Through the Philippians' prayers. (2) Through the help of the Spirit of Jesus Christ. The Philippians' prayers are heard and answered by the Lord, the Great Deliverer. They pray in faith, by the power of the Holy Spirit, who strengthens both Paul and the Philippians to trust in God's provision and deliverance.

2. Jesus prepares them to bear witness for Him when they're dragged before authorities, letting His followers know they don't need to be anxious about wondering how to speak because the Holy Spirit will teach them and speak through them exactly when needed.

3. In Paul's case, he will either be freed from detainment or released as a martyr from this life, delivered for eternity into the arms of Jesus. Because of the promise of salvation and life eternal, Paul (and every believer) can say with confidence that no matter the outcome of their circumstance, they will be delivered!

4. Jesus has delivered us from the present evil age (**Galatians 1:4**), from the domain of darkness (**Colossians 1:13**), and from the wrath to come (**1 Thessalonians 1:10**). God has transferred us to the kingdom of His beloved Son (**Colossians 1:13**), according to His will (**Galatians 1:4**).

DAY 4

1. Wording will vary. Christ = The one for whom Paul lives. Representing Christ in all we say and do, honoring Him with our lives. Gain = Far better is to be with Christ, departing in death to the fullness of life forever with the Savior.

2. He desires "to depart and be with Christ" (**Philippians 1:23;** see also **2 Corinthians 5:8**) but knows it is better for them if he remains in the body, filled with the Holy Spirit—through whom Christ works, to encourage them toward their growth and progress in faith; to teach and guide them, that their joy may increase, even as they're facing persecution for their faith. As a result of Paul coming to them again, they will glorify God for all He's done for them in Christ!

3. Answers may include His presence, grace, strength, and ability to work all things together for good: "And we know that for those who love God all things work together for good, for those who are called according to His purpose" (**Romans 8:28**).

4. Answers will vary. Maybe another person is impacted by your witness in the midst of (or as a result of) your circumstance. Maybe God will use it to open a door to a new situation, person, or conversation. Take time for prayer.

DAY 5

1. Spirit; striving; opponents

2. The difficult message Paul gives is that they will suffer for Christ, as believers; they will be in conflict with the opposition, as Paul is. They may even face death for their faith. He tells them they don't have to be afraid of the opponents (which implies there's good reason for fear). He's heard they're having the same troubles he had. The opponents' behavior is a clear sign of their destruction (because of their rejection of Christ/the Gospel) and of the believers' salvation from God by faith. They will suffer for His sake—for the sake of the Gospel.

3. Peter and John rejoiced that they were considered worthy to suffer for sharing Christ! We can rejoice that we share Jesus' sufferings as a result of sharing the Gospel; others see its effect on us and God is glorified through us. We are blessed when we are insulted because of our faith in Christ; we are not alone, since the Holy Spirit rests upon us, empowering and working in us, turning insults into blessings. We can consider it pure joy when we have trials, because God will use them to make us increasingly steadfast, mature in the faith, and lacking nothing.

4. When we have joy in our unity with other believers, it shows. United, we lift up and defend one another; we hold one another accountable when tempted to compromise convictions due to opposition. We share encouragement of the best kind! When we're united, agreeing in the Lord, our message is loving and clear, even to those who may despise it.

WEEK 3

DAY 1

1. "In Paul's teaching, this personal union is the basic reality of salvation. To be in Christ is to be saved" (*CSSB*, p. 1818). We are no longer condemned by our sin because Christ lives in us by faith. With new life in the Spirit, we are free from the bondage to sin and death. Rejoice!

2. Encouragement; comfort; Spirit; affection; sympathy.

3. Paul's joy will be complete as believers give to one another what Christ first gave (imitating Christ's example), having the same mind and the same love; being in full agreement (accord) with one another and with "one mind." (Paul is effectively repeating and reinforcing his challenge in 1:27.)

4. The fullness of Jesus' joy is ours as we abide in Him, His Word, and His love—bearing fruit, through which God is glorified. (In the **John 15** verses to follow, we learn the first of that fruit is love for others.) Our joy comes from our unity with Christ, and our joy is full in Him. Joy is "complete" when we're imitating Christ and giving others what He first gave us.

DAY 2

1. Selfish ambition promotes disunity and disharmony. Their motives were self-gain, envy, rivalry; their competitive (rather than cooperative) attitudes and actions stood in direct opposition to the unity and harmony necessary to the health of the whole.

2. Wording may include honor others above yourselves; serve one another in love; submit to one another; clothe/cover yourselves with humility toward one another; "God opposes the proud but gives grace to the humble" (1 **Peter** 5:5).

3. "Walk in a manner worthy of the calling" (1:27a); "humility" (2:3); "in love" (2:2); "the unity of the Spirit" (1:27b). Answers may include the significance of unity flowing out of humility. Personal stories and examples will be unique to each person.

4. No, it does not mean denying our interests entirely. It means giving others priority and preference, humbly putting their needs ahead of ours. Our healthy, God-pleasing interests are often linked to our gifts and the ways we connect with others and serve them. Esteeming others, emboldened by Christ, we want to serve, and that may involve our interests. We are careful to give the same care and concern for the interests of others as we would have for ourselves ("not only, . . . but also").

DAY 3

1a. "Emptied Himself"; "form of a servant"; "born in the likeness of men"; "found in human form"; "humbled Himself"; "obedient to . . . death"

1b. **Matthew 20:28**—form of a servant; **Luke 2:10–11**—born in the likeness of men; **John 1:14**—found in human form; **Romans 8:3**—born in the likeness of men, found in human form; **2 Corinthians 8:9**—emptied himself, humbled himself; **Hebrews 5:7–8**—obedient

2. Serve others. Answers will vary.

3. He interrupted His last meal with them to perform the lowest slave's role: the washing of feet. Jesus set an example of humility for His disciples (all Christians) to follow. If even foot washing was not too menial a service for Jesus, then there is no service too lowly for His disciples (us) to do. This act preceded the next day's ultimate act of sacrificial love and humble service, when Jesus willingly went to the cross, dying in our place for our sins, thereby washing them away!

4. Obedience. Answers will vary.

DAY 4

1. "Highly exalted"; "name . . . above every name"; "every knee should bow"; "every tongue confess"; "Jesus Christ is Lord"

2. Here, too, Paul says Christ is above every other name! God raised up Christ—exalted Him—seated Him at His right hand in heaven, far above every ruler, authority, power, and dominion, and not only now but also in the ages to come. **Hebrews 1:3** says Christ "sat down at the right hand of the Majesty on high."

3a.   Believe; repent and be baptized; preach boldly; ready to be imprisoned or die; call upon Him; assemble (gather with other believers); are washed, sanctified, and justified. Everything we say or do should be done in Jesus' name, giving thanks to God the Father through Him! Jesus is at the center of everything we do. Ultimately, our purpose and our priorities line up with God's will, by His grace.

3b.   Knee should bow; tongue confess. This will happen on the great and glorious day of the Lord, at the second coming of Christ—Judgment Day.

4.   He compares their upcoming sorrow and joy with a woman giving birth: the intense sorrow/anguish at the pain of birth that's quickly forgotten in her joy over this new life! In response to His crucifixion, the disciples will weep and lament, but their sorrow at His death will turn to *joy* at His resurrection. This resurrection *joy* has no end and cannot be taken away (from them or us)! As they ask and receive, according to God's will, their *joy* will be full! After He rises, they will pray directly to the Father, asking everything in Jesus' name; God hears and answers every prayer for Jesus' sake, according to His will. Jesus intercedes for us as we humbly pray in His name (see **Hebrews 7:25**).

Bonus: God the Father is glorified and praised as our love, rooted in knowledge and discernment from His Word, overflows onto others. Covered in Jesus' righteousness, we're made pure and blameless—and ready for Christ's return!

DAY 5

1a.   Turn to God's Word for strength because obedience is difficult, even impossible, on your own. His instructions are for your good and given because He loves you. He knows you cannot obey perfectly on your own. As you bring your failed attempts to Him, He not only forgives and covers you in Christ's perfect peace, but He works greater obedience in you.

1b.   Greater obedience is possible only by His grace and with the Spirit's strength, ever at work in you, making you more Christlike! Repent as the Spirit convicts you through the Word, and seek His strength to resist temptation. It can be scary *and* exciting to follow His lead toward something new; trust Him and follow. Further answers will vary.

2.   "Work out" often means physical exercise, movement, endurance. Here, we exercise our faith as we grow in the Word, move forward in our faith, and express the salvation that is ours by grace through faith. As we endure to the end, we are strengthened continually through the practice of our faith. We're achieving spiritual fitness, along with our brothers and sisters in Christ, our workout partners!

3.   The early believers, like us, are saved by grace through faith alone, of course, but Peter encourages us in our God-given faith to grow in virtue, knowledge, self-control, steadfastness, godliness, brotherly affection, and love. All of this is possible according to God's divine power, who has called us through the Holy Spirit and given us His promises in Christ through His Word. This growth protects believers from ineffectiveness and lack of fruit. Connected to Christ and growing in His Word, we produce fruit by the Spirit, for our growth and effectiveness—for others' good and to God's glory!

4.   Answers will vary.

WEEK 4

DAY 1

1.   a. Our physical action, by God's grace. b. His action/work in us. c. His action/work in us. d. His action/work and our physical action, by His grace.

2.   Earlier, Paul spoke against envy, rivalry, selfish ambition, and conceit (1:15–18; 2:3). Here, he warns against grumbling and disputing. Personal stories and reasons for negative impact will vary; self-serving motives and actions easily lead to disunity because the focus is on self and not others.

3a.   "Crooked and twisted" gives a visual description of those who think, speak, and live lies, having left the straight path of God's truth to pursue lives of willful disobedience and depravity. Add "generation" and it describes the unbelieving world (*CSSB*, p. 1819). Paul's words apply to our generation and every generation since the fall into sin (**Genesis 3**).

3b.   Moses also describes the people as a "crooked and twisted generation," corrupt in their dealings with God and no longer His children because they are blemished.

3c.   Peter exhorted the early believers to be saved from the crooked/unbelieving world around them. Like Paul, he is warning God's children.

4. Even the smallest light appears very brightly! Yes, those seated in darkness would definitely be drawn to it. The light of our good works is seen as it shines before others, and as a result, all eyes are drawn to God!

1. Only by the Holy Spirit's work through God's Word are we able to shine the light of Christ and serve side by side without grumbling against God or one another. Only by grace through faith are we blameless and pure, covered in Christ's perfection. The Word proclaims the truth that in Christ, we are God's children. Holding fast to the truth that gives life, we receive the ability to exercise all parts of this "action plan."

2. Answers will vary. All too easily, we may fall for twisted lies, cleverly disguised as "truth" if we do not know the absolute truth of God's Word. The Gospel itself motivates us to hold fast to the Word, stand upon it, and trust the Spirit's strength and guidance through it.

3. A divided, grumbling, self-serving church could not have stood up under opposition or persecution. That kind of church could not have shined light for Christ to the dark world around them in Philippi. Our world today is really no different. We pray we can be one bright, shining light for Christ, with God's help!

4. Paul says he is certain God will bring to completion the "good work" of salvation He has given to them already, by faith. Paul urges them to cling to God's Word, to remain firm in this faith until Christ comes again. God's work through Paul's labor—bringing them the good news and encouraging them in the faith—would be fully realized at Christ's return. "At the day of Jesus Christ" (1:6); "in the day of Christ" (2:16).

1. They respond to God's mercy by presenting their bodies as a living sacrifice, which means offering up their whole lives for service to the Lord and to other people. Christ's sacrificial death, once for all, replaced the Old Testament law of ongoing animal sacrifice for forgiveness. Our life of service is "holy and acceptable to God" (**Romans 12:1**) just as we are "blameless and innocent" (**Philippians 2:15**) because we're covered in Christ's perfection, by His grace. "Spiritual worship" means we have new life by the power of the Spirit; we worship and glorify God in *everything* we do!

2. *Glad* and *rejoice* appear twice. Paul's purpose is twofold. He rejoices with them in their sacrificial living—Jesus is proclaimed through them! He wants them to rejoice with him over his circumstance because, likewise, Jesus is proclaimed through him (in life or in death). **Bonus:** *Offering* appears two times, stressing that Paul (compared to a drink offering) may be poured out to accompany their service, by faith (their sacrificial offering). His sacrifice accompanies—is poured out upon—theirs; they partner as they both proclaim, spiritually side by side though physically far apart.

3. He knows his suffering, just as his life of labor for the Gospel, is not in vain (**v. 16**)! If he is beaten or martyred for the faith, it is for the spread of the Gospel. The Old Testament drink offering pointed forward to Jesus; Paul knows that even his death will point others to Jesus, so he has willingly offered himself up for the sake of the Gospel with great joy.

4. We contemplate death this way only by faith, trusting the Spirit's work through God's true Word. Jesus abolished death and gives life immortal/eternal. Through His death, He has destroyed the devil, the one who has power over death. In eternity with the Lord, there will be no more death, tears, mourning, or pain.

DAY 4

1. Paul points out that Timothy takes a genuine interest in the Philippians' welfare; he invests in others' lives and puts his Gospel work first. He has proven himself to be wholeheartedly faithful. As a son with his father, he has served with Paul in the work of the Gospel. Paul's commendation had little to do with Timothy's personal strengths and everything to do with his others-first, giving heart of service.

2a. Answers will vary.

2b. Answers will vary.

3. (1) Paul is anxious to hear how the Philippians are doing, and he is confident that he will be "cheered" by news of them when Timothy reports back about Paul's "beloved" (**2:12**). He lists this reason before the next, placing them first in priority! (2) Paul knows the Church in Philippi has been waiting eagerly to hear the outcome of his trial. Timothy can't go until he has news to share of Paul's trial's completion, and Paul is hopeful that will be soon. He is almost certain God's plans include his acquittal and release. He trusts "in the Lord"—according to the Lord's will—that he will come to Philippi soon too.

4a. Joy-flood stories will vary.

4b. (1) We serve because we are members of the same body. We each have tasks unique to us. The body works to the fullest when all parts are serving and giving to the whole in their role. (2) We serve because Christ lives in us! His Word dwells in us richly. Think of it this way: what we do flows from our vocation's name (as in, teachers teach). We're all given the name *Christian*: "little Christ." We serve because Christ serves, and He lives in us. (3) We serve in His name, which changes how we look at what we do. When we teach, admonish, sing, or do "whatever" in the name of Jesus, we do it with special purpose, and we glorify Him (taken from Pastor Cory Burma's sermon; used with permission).

DAY 5

1. Paul describes Epaphroditus as his (1) brother, (2) fellow worker, (3) fellow soldier, (4) the Philippians' messenger, and (5) minister to his need. The first three build upon one another. He is more than a brother and more than a worker; he is also a soldier for the Gospel. Paul has great respect for dear Epaphroditus! The last two endear Epaphroditus to his family of faith; he is in Rome on their behalf, as both messenger of their gifts and minister to Paul's needs. He's not just Paul's assistant but is also the church's commissioned and appointed minister.

2. Epaphroditus has been longing for them. He's concerned about them over himself, because word has come back to him that they are distressed about him, having heard he was ill. His longing is likely so they can see for themselves that he's alive and healing, so they may not continue to be distressed. It's believed that Epaphroditus had traveling companions when he was sent to Rome; he had become ill before they left Rome to return home, and he knew they would report this to the believers (Lenski, p. 821).

3. His mercy was demonstrated to Epaphroditus as He provided healing, and to Paul through this healing, that he would be spared "sorrow upon sorrow" (**Philippians 2:27**). The sorrow Paul felt over Epaphroditus's illness didn't diminish his joy, but he is relieved to not bear the additional sorrow he would have endured if his brother had died (Lenski, p. 822).

4. Paul is not upset with them at all. Piggybacking on what we've learned already, the church sent Epaphroditus as a messenger on their behalf. Their service only "lacked" unavoidably, due to the sheer inability of the entire church to travel to Rome. Their commissioned minister came to fill the gap in their service, much as we may send a short-term missionary to assist a career missionary in the field today. Again, Paul honors Epaphroditus in the service he has given; he is complete in his *desire* to carry out what his illness has prevented.

WEEK 5

DAY 1

1. Words of rejoicing, thanks, and praise will be unique to each person.

2. He has written to them or told them these things (in the verses ahead) before, perhaps even face-to-face during his time with them in Philippi. Not only is it no trouble for him to tell them again but also the repetition is for their protection! We can proceed (and we will in tomorrow's reading), knowing there are warnings ahead.

3. Suffering → Endurance → Character → Hope. Stories and answers will be unique to each person. We can look at suffering through Christ and not lose hope because He redeems our experiences . . . and us, by the power of the Holy Spirit!

4. Answers will vary. Happiness is a feeling; joy is a fruit of the Spirit, a gift of God by faith.

DAY 2

1a. Since they're all conditional, if we've rooted all our confidence in them, we could find ourselves devastated or devoid of all confidence if they change or disappear.

1b. Possible destroyers of conditional confidence: failure; criticism; lack of necessary/new abilities; lack of education needed; change in appearance; failing health; loss of possessions; loss of job or demotion; damaged or broken relationships; lack of knowledge.

2. Wording may include the following for each line, after the key word and phrase. Worship—The Holy Spirit produces faith in us; we live a life of worship of the one triune God, who has chosen and redeemed us! Glory—He is glorified by our worship; He's the only one who can save us! No confidence—We place no trust in the flesh, no trust in human effort for salvation; instead, we trust solely in Christ and His work for us!

3. Circumcised; tribe of Benjamin; Hebrew of Hebrews; Pharisee; persecutor; righteous.

4. Go straight to God's Word to receive affirmation and answers through these verses.

DAY 3

1. Some examples: self-centered, self-promotion, self-absorbed, self-esteem, self-awareness, self-image, self-help, self-worth, self-care. (Note that some examples are selfish in nature; others are healthy, like self-care.) Answers will vary. There's a healthy place to think of self, as we seek, in the Spirit's strength, to be self-forgetful, selfless, even self-sacrificing in our thoughts, words, and interactions, but we're also not meant to be self-abasing (belittling or degrading ourselves). All this said, our sinful nature would have us look to ourselves first, and self-confidence has no place in our salvation. We can, however, be confident in our daily walk when we know whose we are and where our strength comes from. "*I can do all things through Him who strengthens me*" (**Philippians 4:13**)!

2. **Left column:** gain; everything; rubbish; Law. **Right column:** loss; knowing; found; faith. Paul doesn't mince words! He uses these contrasting words as an urgent warning against the despicable practices of the Judaizers.

3. Our confidence/trust is in the Lord. We will have seasons of difficulty, struggles, and doubt, with little to no refreshment in sight; especially then, we rely on the deep roots we have in Christ for continued sustenance and strength. We soak up His Word; we flourish, fed by His grace so we can continue to bear fruit, the good work He has for us! Only as a branch is connected to the vine can it bear fruit; we remain connected to Christ and bear His fruit (see **John 15**).

4. Personalization of verses will vary. *Beauty* = Your real beauty comes from within the heart; this beauty is imperishable, does not fade, and lasts forever; it is very precious in God's sight. *Identity* = God created you, redeemed/saved you, and calls you by name; He says to you, "You are Mine!" He loves you so much, He calls you His child—and you are! You are a child of God through faith, baptized into Christ. *Value* = Not conditional, not by achievements or abilities. You are so valuable to Him; you were bought with the ultimate price—Christ's life—and you are chosen in Him.

DAY 4

1. One name for God that defines Him, in part, is "The LORD is our righteousness" (**Jeremiah 23:6**). The righteousness of God is given through faith in Jesus to all who believe. Although we're sinners, we are justified—made right with God—by the gift of God's grace given through Jesus' death for us (redemption for our sins). This shows God's righteousness, the justifier of all who have faith in Jesus (**Romans 3:21–26**). Righteousness is ours only by the grace of God; if it came by the Law, "then Christ died for no purpose" (**Galatians 2:21**).

2. NOT . . . *my own; from the Law.* BUT . . . *from God; by faith.* A righteousness by my own doing/attempt that comes from the Law is impossible to attain; because of sin, I cannot follow the Law with the perfection God requires (Lenski, p. 839). Only He is perfectly righteous. A righteousness from God is His doing—His action on my behalf at Christ's cross that comes by faith. Because of Christ, I'm righteous through faith. Not only is this possible, it's a reality!

3. This message is of utmost importance; it must be deeply and repeatedly rooted in every believer. To confuse or muddy the Law with the Gospel is to negate Christ's full and complete work for us—it's to deny the Gospel's purity and power for life and salvation! And because of our sinful nature and the trappings of our world, there will always be a temptation and tendency to slip into the way of thinking that says we must do something to be made right with God. But God is clear: "the righteous shall live by faith" (**Romans 1:17**)!

4. We know good works can't save us, but there's a place for them! By God's grace, we are saved through faith and not by works. We cannot earn our salvation. (Remember, the very definition of grace is unearned, undeserved favor!) Because of faith, however, works naturally result! We are God's workmanship—His masterpiece creations! And our works, which He prepared in advance for us, are our response to His saving grace, by the outpouring of the Holy Spirit.

DAY 5

1. Stories of God's power at work will be unique to each person. Maybe the topic of your morning devotion was just what you needed for direction later in the day; maybe the Scripture from a sermon gave you the discernment you needed for a difficult situation; maybe you've watched a miracle unfold, following fervent prayer!

2. Imprisonments, beatings, thirty-nine lashes five times, stoned, shipwrecked; in danger from rivers, robbers, from his own people and from Gentiles; in danger in the city, the wilderness, at sea, and from false brothers. Toil, hardship, sleepless nights, hunger and thirst, in cold and exposure. Anxiety for the believers (**2 Corinthians 11:23–28**). Weaknesses, insults, hardships, persecutions, and calamities (**2 Corinthians 12:10**). Recall that when he was with them in Philippi, they saw his beatings and then chains in the Philippian jail. (See **Acts 16**.)

3. We will be glorified with Christ when we are united with Him in heaven and His glory is then fully revealed to us. That glory will far outweigh all suffering—the two are not even worth comparing. Suffering today may mean being mocked by skeptics and unbelievers and sometimes even ridiculed or insulted by churches who misuse, water down, or pervert the Gospel. It may mean job loss, hate mail, even death threats due to our profession of faith. Other answers will vary, as persecution takes many different forms. Through Peter, God says we can rejoice in suffering, and we will rejoice again when His glory is fully revealed in us at the final resurrection.

4. Answers may include these: Since Jesus died and rose again, God will bring with Him all who have fallen asleep in death. Jesus will descend from heaven and those who died in faith will rise first. Those who are still living on the day of Christ's return will be caught up with those who have risen and all will meet the Lord in the air. All believers will be with the Lord forever.

WEEK 6

1. The brothers (and sisters) in Christ might think too high-
    ly of Paul, that he is somehow complete or already made
    perfect; someone who could reproach others but no longer
    needed it himself. Lesser men than Paul have convinced
    themselves that they have achieved perfection in this life
    and have persuaded followers to believe it too, thus damag-
    ing everyone involved (Lenski, p. 848).

2. Paul *strains forward* and *presses on* toward the *goal* for the
    prize; these words provide the imagery of a race. He runs his
    hardest, aiming for the prize, to win the race. Training and
    running involve constant discipline and self-control, never
    running aimlessly, but steadily toward the goal; not falling
    away or falling into sin, but single-mindedly carrying the
    Gospel forward.

3. The prize is Jesus Himself, who promised to raise believers
    up on the Last Day. We receive bodily resurrection—and
    we're made perfect—when Christ returns and we receive an
    imperishable body and life forever with Him!

4. Paul does not let the past negatively impact his run for
    Christ with the Gospel. He knows his former life is behind
    him, done, and forgiven. Reflecting in a healthy way upon
    the past could enable us to learn from it and release it, with
    God's help. He has removed our sins from us as far as the
    east is from the west. He doesn't hold our sins against us,
    so neither should we! We can confess them, trusting God
    removes them.

DAY 2

1. "Also" implies that God was the one who revealed to the
    mature believers all the knowledge of Christ they possess
    already—all that had brought them to their maturity, by the
    power of the Spirit at work through His Word and the apos-
    tles (Lenski, p. 854).

2. Circle: as you received Christ Jesus the Lord. Underline:
    walk in Him; rooted; built up in Him; established in the
    faith; abounding in thanksgiving. (Even "taught" speaks to
    growth.) Star: captive by philosophy and empty deceit; hu-
    man tradition; elemental spirits of the world; not according
    to Christ. Dangers: Worldly teachings are powerless to ex-
    plain God adequately; we're deceived if we think they can.
    All of this is opposed to Christ!

3. Stories and answers will vary.

4. They equip the saints/believers, as all believers have a role in the work of ministry. The purpose is to build up the Body of Christ so all attain unity of faith and the fullness of the knowledge of Christ to maturity! Growing (through the teaching) to maturity wards against being swayed or fooled by false doctrine. We grow up as the Body of Christ so it works as one, under the Head of Christ.

DAY 3

1. Imitate those who have received the Word in affliction with joy; those who are not idle or sluggish but labor to pay their own way so as not to burden others; those who through faith and patience inherit God's promises. Imitate the faith of leaders who have spoken the Word of God to you. Imitate good, not evil. Personal examples will vary.

2. You get to witness, firsthand, the blessings and fruits coming from someone whose eyes are on the prize; you see how a person of faith handles difficulties; you learn godly responses as opposed to worldly reactions; you see someone who gives grace when needed and redirection when necessary. Examples and reasons will vary.

3. Stories and answers will vary. Maybe they will imitate your habit of going to God's Word for answers and going to His house for worship. Maybe your listening skills, patience, prayer life, or passion are worthy of imitation.

4. It's important to remember that every believer, no matter how mature, is saint *and* sinner at the same time. The most mature Christians still sin, imperfect this side of heaven. If we follow anyone blindly, we may be tempted to justify their mistakes. That said, with our eyes wide open, we have so much to gain from a godly example!

DAY 4

1. Salvation = citizenship in heaven; Christ-centered; Glory in Christ (who transforms our bodies to be glorified/imperishable like His); Heavenly things. The contrast is vast; we can see why he is moved to tears as he describes the depth of the enemies' depravity (Lenski, p. 860) and urges the believers to be alert and stand firm.

2. Stated in Colossians and implied in Philippians: your minds "on things that are above" (the place of heavenly citizenship, "where Christ is, seated at the right hand of God" [Colossians 3:1]). Stated in both: "With minds set on earthly

things" (**Philippians 3:19**) and "set your minds . . . not on things that are on earth" (**Colossians 3:2**).

3. Our bodies will be raised imperishable, both spiritual and physical, bearing the image of Christ! Perishable puts on imperishable; mortal puts on immortal. By Jesus' complete and absolute power (the miraculous power that enables Him to subject all things to Himself), He will raise up our dead bodies in glory.

4. Answers may include wholeness of mind, body, and soul. There will be no more mourning or crying or pain (**Revelation 21:4**). Fullness of JOY!

DAY 5

1. Top layer: my brothers; I love and long for; my joy and crown. Bottom layer: my beloved. Meat: stand firm thus in the Lord.

2. Instruction Paul gives to help believers "stand firm" (from 3:12–21):

    Press on, even when facing adversity and opposition.

    Keep your eyes on the prize of Christ—His return and the final resurrection.

    Rest in His confidence; He has made you His own, He has called you, and He is at work in you.

    Look to good examples and imitate them, as they seek to imitate Christ.

    Be alert to those who pervert the Gospel or live as though they have a license to do whatever they want (their god is their stomach; they glory in shame; their minds are on earthly things).

    Have your mind on heavenly things over earthly matters.

    Wait eagerly for Christ's return, knowing your real citizenship is in heaven.

    Know He will transform your body to be imperishable—glorified—like His.

    All of this is by His power! All things are under Him (3:21).

    From this list, responses will vary, regarding which instruction currently stands out most.

3. Answers will vary.

4. **2 Thessalonians 2:14–15:** God has called you through the Gospel; He enables you to *stand firm*! Hold to the traditions—the established Christian teaching and doctrine—without any alteration (*TLSB*, p. 2063). **2 Timothy 4:3–5:** *Stand firm* when people around you stray away from truth. Be sober-minded and endure suffering as you do the work of an evangelist. (Paul is speaking to Timothy as a fellow pastor, but this can be applied to us in our vocations.) **Romans 12:2:** *Stand firm*, not allowing yourself to be conformed to this world; be transformed by the renewal of your mind, through God's Word (the means by which we know His good, acceptable, and perfect will).

WEEK 7

DAY 1

1. The Holy Spirit provides unity, working powerfully through believers (even when it doesn't seem possible!). Paul urges them to let their lives be consistent with the Gospel, to stand firm in the unity of the Spirit, striving side by side as they live and share the Gospel by faith. He urges them to be of the same mind, united as one in Christ! He urges the women to set aside their differences, to "agree in the Lord" (**Philippians 4:2**), to be united!

2. The women did not keep the disagreement between themselves. The disagreement was sizable enough for Paul to gently and briefly address it publicly in his letter. Paul is impartial and does not take sides but mentions the women equally; we can assume both had a role in the disagreement. He refrains from speaking negatively with "don't" or "stop" but appropriately asks them to "agree in the Lord" (4:2). He asks those closest to the women to help them reconcile. They had once worked side by side with Paul to advance the Gospel, and here we believe they've continued. They are true believers, along with Clement (not mentioned elsewhere) and all the fellow workers for the Gospel.

3. Names and prayers will be unique to each person. Answers may include being the first to take the initiative toward improved and healthy communication.

4. "Finally, brothers, rejoice. Aim for restoration, comfort one another, agree with one another, live in peace; and the God of love and peace will be with you" (**2 Corinthians 13:11**). Answers will vary.

DAY 2

1. Specific circumstances will vary. "The light [Christ] shines in the darkness, and the darkness has not overcome it" (**John 1:5**). Remember this: light dispels darkness and the light of Christ shines *on* you and *in* you . . . even *through* you to others! Even the darkness is not dark to the Lord; the night's as light as day because He *is* light and life, and He is with you.

2. Circumstances and answers are unique to each person, of course. (Maybe a rough patch in a relationship, a cross-country or local move, a career change, a time of personal crisis in the workplace, a difficult semester in school, a health scare, a loss or permanent life change.) It's not unusual to feel stripped of joy in the toughest of times; remember to trust the Truth whenever your feelings attempt to betray you. No one and nothing can steal your joy!

3. Answers will vary, but may include being mindful, gentle, slow to anger, thoughtful, caring, compassionate, generous, considerate, patient, and quick to forgive and reconcile.

4. In light of eternity and Christ's imminent return, we give priority to our relationships, with concern for them and Christlike treatment of them, by God's grace. We are moved to rejoice! He could return in our lifetime—anytime. You and I are to live just as the first readers of this letter, with joyful expectation that His return is near. Come quickly, Lord Jesus (**Revelation 22:20**).

DAY 3

1. Here is a compiled list of responses from a number of women: pressures of life, deadlines, weight/health, family, children, aging parents, finances, job security, job/co-worker/boss issues, national security, economic crisis, provision for family, sharing the Gospel, friendships/relationships, spiritual welfare of loved ones, overwhelmed, becoming a parent, big decisions, acceptance.

2. *Nothing!* There's an appropriate place for concern—not anxiety—when we need to be proactive, to take action when appropriate and possible. This shouldn't, however, give us justification for anxiety over issues beyond our control or an unhealthy preoccupation over a circumstance that may never happen. For example, with a history of a specific health condition in the family, concern would tell us to get regular checkups. Consider, too, the valid cause for concern that Paul had for Epaphroditus's health, when he mentions

sending him home, so he (Paul) may be "less anxious" (**Philippians 2:28**).

3. *Everything!* God knows exactly what we need before we ask Him (**Matthew 6:8**), but He wants us to ask! Where better could we take every care, concern, and anxiety than to the One who knows them already and answers our every prayer? If not with a "yes" then with "I have something even better; trust Me." He answers every prayer according to His will—see **1 John 5:14–15**.

4. Stories will be unique to each person. Although we may not fully understand how we can experience peace in the midst of suffering or difficult circumstances, we humbly, joyfully receive it by God's grace through faith in Jesus.

DAY 4

1. Answers will vary. Take time for confession and prayer.

2. True: false, lies. Honorable: shameful, detestable. Just: wrong, unjust, dishonest. Pure: tainted, corrupt. Lovely: nasty, unpleasant. Commendable: unworthy, contemptible, worthless. Excellent: poor, deficient. Worthy of Praise: blameworthy, guilty.

3. Answers will vary.

4. If we test our thoughts against these values from God's Word, He will reveal when our runaway thoughts need to be taken captive and made obedient to Christ. We seek His forgiveness and strength to turn our thoughts to be in line with these ideals.

DAY 5

1. (1) Learned; (2) received; (3) heard; (4) seen. "These things" have been lived out by Paul and personally shared again and again with the Philippians. *Learned and received:* Paul brought them the Gospel face-to-face and continues to teach them God's Word from afar through this letter, through Epaphroditus, and in his ongoing partnership in the Gospel with them. *Heard and seen:* He has been an example to them through both his words and his life.

2. Examples will be unique to each person.

3. Circle "whatever" in **verses 17** and **23**. As believers, our lives are united with Christ; everything we think, say, and do is connected to Him! "There's no division between the sacred and the secular concerning what a Christian says and does" (*TLSB*, p. 2048). Wording may vary for the following answers:

May all I say (word) and do (deed) be done in Jesus' name!

May I give thanks to God the Father through Jesus.

May I work heartily ("from the soul" [*TLSB*, p. 2048]) in all I do, as if I'm working for the Lord and not for people; I receive an inheritance, salvation by faith, from the Lord.

May I remember that in serving others I'm ultimately serving Christ.

4. (1) He will be with us. (2) He is the God of peace who gives peace. The promises of God's presence and peace sustain and strengthen us! He never leaves our side, and He fills us with peace for today and eternity.

WEEK 8

DAY 1

1. They finally have opportunity to show their ongoing concern and care for Paul with the gift Epaphroditus brought. Their love of him is shown in active giving, evidence that God's love in Christ flows through them. In addition, their continued growth in unity and humility, their perseverance in hardships, and their partnership with Paul are further evidence of the Gospel's work in their lives.

2. One extreme: abound, plenty, abundance. The other: brought low, hunger, need. Material provisions alone cannot provide real contentment. Riches may leave a person merely longing for more.

3. Notes about the verses will vary, but may include His power is made perfect in weakness; I'll boast of my weakness, that His power may rest on me; I can be content in weakness and hardships because of His power; when I am weak, then I am strong (from **2 Corinthians 12**). I am strengthened with power through His Spirit in me; Christ dwells in my heart through faith (from **Ephesians 3**). I am strengthened by His power and glorious might for endurance and patience with joy (from **Colossians 1**).

4. Answers may include these: I can live with joy, peace, and contentment in times of plenty OR want, in hardship OR good times. I can persevere with His strength, holding on in any circumstance because His power rests upon me and fills me.

1. Their gift reveals the depth of their faith, their devotion to the Lord and His salvation work. This beautiful fruit produced in the believers causes Paul to rejoice!

2. God's grace had been given to them and was working mightily through them! In **2 Corinthians 8:1–5**, Paul says they gave in the midst of "a severe test of affliction"; with "a wealth of generosity" and "abundance of joy," even in their "extreme poverty." They gave "beyond their means," "of their own accord," even "begging earnestly" to take part first in a relief effort for other believers and then specifically for Paul and his companions, by God's will.

3. As believers who live their lives for Christ as living sacrifices, they are producing the Spirit's fruit! They've given their offering out of their poverty and beyond their means—sacrificially. God is glorified in their gift-giving—yet another pleasing aroma! (Their gift to Paul is really an offering to God!) (Lenski, p. 896). In **Ephesians 5:2**, the fragrant offering is Christ, who gave Himself up for us as a sacrifice to God—once for all. In **2 Corinthians 2:14–15**, fragrance refers to the aroma of Christ we spread as we share the knowledge of Him everywhere. Christ is the ultimate fragrant offering for forgiveness and salvation; believers (then and now!) spread this fragrance when we share the Gospel. As we offer up our bodies, lives, and gifts, may they be fragrant offerings too, pleasing to the Lord because of Christ's sacrifice *for* us and God's work *in* us.

4. Connections often develop even further, after a time of generous giving and gracious receiving. Giving *and* receiving bless us in so many ways! Giving can help us release our grip on things and even increase our faith as we see the effect our generosity has on the recipient. When we receive graciously, our needs are met *and* we bring joy to the giver, especially as she sees our joy-filled response and knows that she's making a difference. (Joy flows both ways!)

1a. Listed items may include food, clothing, and shelter. Relationships, communication, and quiet time may be examples of emotional needs. Forgiveness, grace, peace, and joy are all spiritual needs, to name a few.

1b. Prayerfully consider all listed needs, for discernment about those that may need to go. Take time for prayer, and praise the One who supplies all your needs.

2. Answers will vary. The reason I believe Jesus is my only real need is that when I have Jesus (and I do, by God's grace, through His gift of faith!), everything else either fails in contrast or follows in connection with Him, as part of His provision. He is the great provider for ALL my needs, so He is all I need! Examples of other faith-based one-liners: *Exercise daily—walk with God! Christian under Construction. Jesus is the anchor in my storms.*

3. Underline: receive Him; believed in His name; He gave the right to become; born . . . of God (by faith); received the Spirit of adoption as sons; the Spirit Himself bears witness. Highlight: children of God, sons, Abba, Father, children, heirs, fellow heirs (co-heirs with Christ). Answers may include feelings of awe, wonder, and joy that God knows and cares for you so personally and completely.

4. We are made righteous by faith and produce the Spirit's fruit in our lives, which gives God glory (1:11). He is glorified, too, as we confess Jesus is Lord (2:11)! God receives glory in your life as you praise and worship Him with fellow believers *and* as you lift your life to Him daily. By His grace, may you be mindful of His presence, provision, and power in your life. Personal answers will vary.

DAY 4

1. The believers are asked to greet one another with a holy kiss. In their culture, a holy kiss was as common among Christians as a handshake or a warm embrace is in ours. In Jesus' parable of the prodigal son (**Luke 15**), the father embraced the son with a kiss. When Paul left Ephesus (**Acts 20**), his tear-filled departure included embraces and kisses from the elders. Some modern churches exchange the holy kiss of peace, according to their culture, much as my church shares peace with a handshake and a few words.

2. No matter what service is like under Nero, they're sure to have found joy in their opportunities to interact with Paul. This long-awaited trial brings not only Paul's case forward but the cause of the Gospel as a whole. "Who would now be more concerned than these slaves of Nero's own household?" (Lenski, p. 900).

3. In **Luke 1:26–38**, the angel Gabriel *greets* Mary in her home to tell her she has found favor with God; she will bear a Child and become the mother of her Savior, Jesus! Mary responds first in fear, "greatly troubled," but after the angel explains how this will happen and what it will mean, Mary *responds* obediently and later *rejoices* with a song of praise (1:46–55). Immediately following Mary's encounter with the angel, in **Luke 1:39–45**, Mary *greets* her cousin Elizabeth at her home. Immediately, the baby in Elizabeth's womb leaps for *joy*; filled with the Holy Spirit, Elizabeth *responds* with great *rejoicing*! In **Matthew 28**, the risen Jesus *greets* Mary Magdalene and the other Mary outside the tomb. They're already filled with *joy* following the angel's news, and now the Lord Himself greets them face-to-face! The women *respond*, bowing to His feet and worshiping Him.

4. Answers will vary. Maybe you give a nod or warm word, or you call them by name. Maybe you offer a handshake, a hug, or even a holy kiss. Expressing "I'm glad to see you and greet you with the peace of Jesus!" can welcome someone and keep them "coming back."

DAY 5

1. *Grace* and *the Lord Jesus Christ*. (Best words ever!) In Paul's opening greetings, he proclaims the blessing of grace and peace *from* the Father and His Son, our Savior. In the closing benediction, he pronounces the blessing *of* the grace of our Savior, Jesus, to be with our spirit.

2. Wording may include the following: *Faith* = Belief in God's promise of salvation in Christ, by the Holy Spirit's power (**Acts 16:31**—Paul's words to the jailer in Philippi!); we're justified by this faith, which gives us peace with God; we live by faith in the one who gave Himself for us. *Hope* = Jesus is our hope! By God's grace, we have a living hope in Christ; a confident trust in Him; certainty of our salvation. *Comfort* = To encourage; to feel compassion for another and care for them. God gives us comfort so we can give His comfort to others. Additional answers about the impact of these gifts will vary. Other gifts might include compassion, strength, and contentment.

3. Answers will vary.

4. Stories will be unique to each person. Ideas to help remember may include posting "God leans in" somewhere you'll see it daily, along with verses about His strength (start with **Philippians 4:13**!). Ideas may also include prayer for the person, the situation, and yourself; for the ability to place yourself in their "shoes."

Bibliography

Bordeleau, Jessica. *5 Meaningful Minutes for Moms*. Fenton, MO: CTA, Inc. 2017. Used with permission grant #091818. © 2017 CTA, Inc. www.CTAinc.com.

Burma, Deb. *Raising Godly Girls*. St. Louis: Concordia Publishing House, 2015.

———. *Stepping Out: To a Life on the Edge*. St. Louis: Concordia Publishing House, 2013.

Corzine, Jacob A. "Joy in Adversity," *Portals of Prayer* 81, no. 440 (July–September 2018): August 21.

———. "Thy Will Be Done," *Portals of Prayer* 81, no. 440 (July–September 2018): August 28.

Engelbrecht, Edward A., ed. *Concordia's Complete Bible Handbook*, second edition. St. Louis: Concordia Publishing House, 2013.

———, ed. *Lutheran Bible Companion*, vol. 2. St. Louis: Concordia Publishing House, 2014.

———, ed. *The Lutheran Study Bible*. St. Louis: Concordia Publishing House, 2009.

Eschelbach, Michael. *The Big Book of New Testament Questions and Answers*. St. Louis: Concordia Publishing House, 2015.

Floyd, Heidi. *In a Word: Quiet Little Thoughts about God*. St. Louis: Concordia Publishing House, 2011.

Fryar, Jane L. *Today's Light Devotional Bible*. St. Louis: Concordia Publishing House, 2014.

Geisler, Dr. Carol A. "For the Record," *Portals of Prayer* 81, no. 440 (July–September 2018): September 24.

Gernant Dumit, Julene. *Philippians: Joy in Christ*. God's Word for Today. St. Louis: Concordia Publishing House, 1997.

Hawthorne, Gerald F. *Philippians*. Word Biblical Commentary, vol. 43. Waco, TX: Word, 1983. Copyright © 1983 by Word, Inc. Used by permission of Thomas Nelson. www.thomasnelson.com.

Hoerber, Robert G., ed. *Concordia Self-Study Bible*. St. Louis: Concordia Publishing House, 1986.

Lenski, R. C. H. *Interpretation of Galatians, Ephesians, Philippians.* Columbus, OH: The Wartburg Press, 1946. Used by permission of Augsburg Press, content holder. www.fortresspress.com.

Meyer, Dale A. *Timely Reflections: A Minute a Day with Dale Meyer.* Anaheim Hills, CA: Tri-Pillar Publishing, 2014. Text © 2014 by Dale A. Meyer. Used with permission. www.tripillarpublishing .com.

Pyle, Donna. *Quenched: Christ's Living Water for a Thirsty Soul.* St. Louis: Concordia Publishing House, 2014.

Rau, Andy. "Where Do Verse and Chapter Numbers in the Bible Come From?" *Bible Gateway* (blog). December 20, 2016. www .biblegateway.com/blog/2016/12/where-do-verse-and-chapter-numbers-come-from/.

Smith, Tyler. "In Memory of Elisabeth Elliot: 30 of Her Most Inspiring Quotes." *Logos Talk* (blog). June 15, 2015. blog.logos .com/2015/06/in-memory-of-elisabeth-elliot-30-of-her-most-inspiring-quotes/.

Swindoll, Luci. *Simple Secrets to a Happy Life.* Nashville: Thomas Nelson, 2012. Copyright © 2012 by Luci Swindoll. Used by permission of Thomas Nelson. www.thomasnelson.com.

Personal stories, quotes, memoir (Carol), newsletter (Sarah), and sermon (Pastor Burma) all shared with permission.